Virtual Tour Profit

How to automatically attract high ticket clients, sell subscriptions, and build a wildly profitable VR agency.

Zach Calhoon

Copyright © 2021 Zach Calhoon

All rights reserved.

CONTENTS

	Acknowledgments	i
	Introduction	1
1	The New Virtual Selling Economy	16
2	Foundations - The Insider Truth of Every Transaction	34
3	The VR Digital Media Business Model	55
4	Engineering Awareness: The Five Levels	76
5	How to Charge High Ticket Prices For Your Virtual Tours	86
6	How to Sell Recurring Subscriptions For Your Virtual Tours	95
7	Creating Freedom	111
8	The Importance Of One Niche	124
9	Using Google Maps To Convert The Best Customers	138
10	Advertising That Converts	148
11	The Case Study Valut	160

ACKNOWLEDGMENTS

Shout out to my partner Clayton Rothschild. You have built the best 360° virtual tour platform in the world.

A bigger shoutout to our wives, Michelle and Caroline. Thanks for letting us build this business and always supporting our wild ideas.

Introduction

Virtual Tour Profit

Welcome! We're about to go on a life-changing journey. Are you ready?

My name is Zach Calhoon, I'm the co-founder of CloudPano.com and Virtual Tour Profit. Thank you for grabbing this book – I appreciate your time. There's a lot to cover as we dive into 360° virtual tour technology and learn how to build a robust business that brings repeatable sales. If you stick with me, I will take you from beginner to expert in 11 chapters. You'll have all the tools you need to build an exciting and lucrative virtual tour business.

Virtual Tour Profit

Let's look at what to expect…

First, we'll lay out the 360°/VR economy, what's working now, and how the world is rapidly changing. I will unpack this new opportunity and share how to leverage VR technology to build a dream business.

Whether you sell 360° tech, or you just want to close more sales, I will unpack some helpful frameworks that work for me and our community. You will learn how to get into the mind of your clients and learn their needs. When you become a trusted advisor, selling becomes an easy and fun conversation. Let's remove the pain of selling and build offers that convert!

Then I am going to unpack the VR digital media business model. What offers can you architect inside your digital media business that are not only 360° related, but also come together synergistically to help your clients solve their painful problems? I'll teach you how to engineer awareness through the 5 Levels of Awareness framework. Once you understand these, you'll know what language to use, how to say it and when to close each sale.

I will cover how to acquire high ticket clients. How to make more money per transaction, and how to raise the value of your offer. You will learn how to approach large institutions with virtual tour tech. You will learn how to speak high ticket and solve large enterprise and institutional problems. You will be signing contracts larger than you ever thought possible. Plus, I will show you case studies of CloudPano users who are successfully building tours for clients well above the $10K clip per transaction. You can do this too…

I am also going to teach you how to sell subscriptions for monthly recurring revenue – important stuff! I am going to show you business models, the math, and how to think long term about your business model and strategy. This section has the power to completely change the structure of your offers.

You'll learn how to outsource, how to create freedom in your business, and how to build an entire machine that runs your fulfillment. When you have a team of contractors that you can rely on, you are in a position to scale your business. As your niche reveals more needs, you can say "yes" to more services and hire as needed to get the job done. You will become the only trusted resource needed for your clients.

I will also teach you the important focus of picking one niche. You will learn the advantage of not "serving everyone." When you narrow your focus, your creativity and sales framework become razor sharp. As you begin to prospect and speak to your niche, you will quickly reuse your sales assets and your sales process becomes simple and repeatable.

To accelerate your progress, I will also dive deeper into granular tools to help you find your footing with the small business owner (a great and endless niche to target). You will learn how to use Google Maps to sell more clients. You will learn to leverage Google My Business to get more customers. As you use these tools, you can plug them into your existing business or even have them become offers within your rolodex.

I'll show you how to advertise and write sales copy that converts. As you learn to attract customers, the words you use will be calculated and precise.

Finally, we'll look at a case study vault and examples, sharing stories of CloudPano Pro Plus users and the VTPS community – a good dose of real-world inspiration!

What is CloudPano.com?

CloudPano.com is a 360° virtual tour software. CloudPano was built so VR entrepreneurs can succeed. I am the co-founder – along with Clayton Rothschild (the mad scientist behind every feature). Each feature within

Virtual Tour Profit

CloudPano was built so the VR entrepreneur can make more money.

We built this software as a tool and a resource so you can accelerate and explode in your local context with quick revenue. And we built the software so it's simple to use and understand. This provides clarity as you sell to your clients.

Clayton and I, and our team at CloudPano, have a unique perspective on virtual tours. We see tens of thousands of them come through the platform. We see industries trending and thriving. We have many creative entrepreneurs creating some amazing virtual tours with our platform, and we're able to see everything from a top-level view.

With that in mind, the data, the user base, and having seen globally the new trend of virtual tours, we have clarity. Our ideas aren't pie-in-the-sky or theoretical. The advice I give in this book is from actual experience, both my own and the experience of our users. CloudPano is a true passion of mine – a life calling. We have a large, dedicated team that works every day to make it the best platform in the world. We do it with passion and heart and ultimately, we do it for you. We want you to succeed. YOUR success is OUR success!

Virtual Tour Profit

A Challenge to Start Today

For a moment, I'd like to give you a challenge. Make a promise to yourself to work your way through all 11 chapters. I understand it's easy to get distracted along the way. But you've picked up this book because you want to excel at building a new income stream and build a robust business that lasts. You want to be an expert and you want to thrive. The only way to really succeed in life is to finish what you start. Push through and read it from cover to cover.

We start off easy (very simple) and pick up the pace and complexity as we dive into the details. If you're already an experienced 360°/VR entrepreneur, stick with me! I have taken great care to make this an easy read, with explanations and examples that you can relate to.

So, with all that said...let's get started! Let's go build a VR digital media agency together. Let's get some customers, put some money in the bank, and have some fun!

Zach Calhoon
Co-Founder – CloudPano.com

A practical note on 360° cameras, photography, and workflows

As I write this book, there is nothing changing faster than the hardware that captures 360° photos. A few short years ago it was very difficult to create a 360° photo and required a cumbersome process of stitching the photos together. Now, through single shot 360° cameras, you can capture a 360° photo in seconds. When the photo is taken, it's captured with two 180° photos with two fisheye lenses. These two photos are stitched in the app and saved on your phone's camera roll as a 360° photo. You can easily upload these photos into CloudPano directly from your phone. And on the Appstore there is a CloudPano 360° app that captures 360° photos of a room and lets you create 360° photos and virtual tours all from your phone. Where this process can get complicated and slows down your learning curve is in the photo post processing stage. If you desire, you can become a post processing expert – get all the tools and software needed – and make your 360° photos look amazing. Depending on your hardware, this workflow may look slightly different, but often this involves tools like photoshop, lightroom, and other third-party optimization tools. Personally, I don't think you should mess with any of these tools (outsource it all) and focus on your business.

Virtual Tour Profit

Here is my point – the hardware will always be changing and there will always be someone who can make your photos look pretty. Don't get lost in this world of "editing" and try to master it before you get started. We will not try to cover the ever changing market of 360° camera hardware and post processing software. Follow the steps laid out in this book, and you will quickly find people to work for you to edit your virtual tours along the way, and they only charge a few dollars per photo.

With all that said… let's get started!

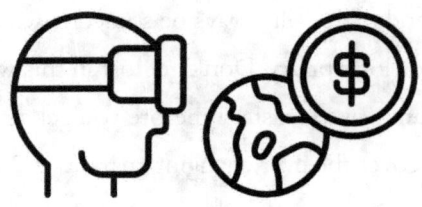

CHAPTER 1

THE NEW VIRTUAL SELLING ECONOMY

The world has shifted to virtual selling – are you ready?

We're at the dawn of a new era.

The summer of 2020 brought with it a pandemic that has changed the world as we know it. A simple trip to the coffee shop meant putting on a mask. To enter a doctor's office meant getting your temperature taken and filling out a form. Millions of people are now working remotely from home and millions were put out of a job as entire industries changed. Industries were forced to shift their marketing and their thinking.

Great change applies pressure to our normal comfort. Those that struggle to adapt will stall, while others who move quickly find new opportunities. And sometimes it's in between these moments in history when fortunes are made. The fact that you've picked up this book shows that you are willing to adapt, change, and grow. My hope is that this book will open your eyes to new opportunities and new creative tech.

Virtual tours and setting up "virtual selling environments" is today's golden opportunity. It helps business owners, entrepreneurs, and enterprises move their inventory, sell their interiors, and show off their space in a world where seeing is believing and "site unseen" virtual buying is the new normal. This is where the new opportunity lies as you look to profit from global change.

I am the co-founder and owner of a successful virtual tour software company called CloudPano, with virtual tours that get over 1 million impressions per day. Early in the pandemic we found ourselves waking up to a shutdown that took place over a few weeks. At first we were not sure what to expect from the market. Quickly as things shut down, virtual selling and 360° tech exploded, and we spiked 10x. We were in the right place at the right time. Users jumped onto our platform and started to make 360° virtual tours for their high demand clients. The marketplace could not go in person - anywhere. So CloudPano took the market to them.

Virtual Tour Profit

This means there's a new global opportunity, and you can take advantage of it. The 360° trend has exploded and it's here to stay. The first movers, the people who move fast and decisively, will be positioned well as other markets adapt to 360° virtual tours and utilize VR experiences. The entrepreneurs who are ready to fulfill those services will be the ones who profit.

For example, one of our CloudPano pro plus members signed a $200,000 contract with a large property management company. Within about three months, she figured out how to create virtual tours. She got resourced so she could fulfill their needs in a professional way. And she sold a large contract to an executive responsible for 30 apartment locations (and new upcoming developments). Of course she delivered world class virtual tours on CloudPano.

Multiple markets (hardware, software, and demand) have all changed and come together at the same time. The stars have aligned. Today it's super simple to create a virtual tour on CloudPano.com. 360° cameras have totally changed as well. In the past, creating a 360° photo required lots of complex post-production, but not anymore. Now it's simpler than ever and actually pretty easy to create a 360° photo. All

Virtual Tour Profit

you need is to place a camera in the center of a room, activate a timer, and within a few seconds it takes a spherical photo that captures the entire space – ceiling to floor and all the doors and windows around it. This 360° image asset is then placed in virtual tour software, and the result is a powerful marketing tool that can be used by clients all over the world to market and sell their stuff.

From properties to cars, churches to boats, there are endless applications for using 360° tours. And as 360° imagery becomes more and more popular, buyers are increasingly learning to expect a 360° tour of the item for sale.

There is a new economy and new markets are opting into the tech as a **must have to win** marketing tool. These shifts in the market have opened up an opportunity to entrepreneurs, and it doesn't require experience or massive effort to get started. Plus, 360° virtual tours plug into the VR world. If you have created a 360° virtual tour, you can view it in a VR headset. This creates a fully immersive experience that is a powerful and formidable marketing tool. To the end client, the production looks complicated, but the creation is simple.

You can charge high prices, sell subscriptions, and build a full business around this concept. Plus, if you have an existing business, it's easy to plug in this service as an additional revenue stream.

WHAT IS A 360° TOUR?

A 360° virtual tour is a sequence of panoramic images that are "stitched" together to create a "virtual" experience of any location. This virtual experience can be viewed through desktop computers, laptops, tablets, and smartphones.

All you need is a 360° photo that you upload into 360° virtual tour software. When your virtual tour is created, it's delivered to the client as a hyperlink, a new URL address.

Here is the process... You start with a 360° camera (or DSLR with a fisheye lens). There is a wide variety of 360° cameras (Ricoh Theta Z1, Insta 360 One X2 etc.) or today you can use your phone with a 360° photo application (search CloudPano in the app store). If you're shooting a property and want to show the interior, the camera is placed in the center of each room. You set a timer for a few seconds (5 to 10 seconds). This gives you enough time to exit the room and click – the photo is taken. Your device stores two spherical photos that are stitched together into one photo file. When these two spherical photos are stitched together, they create a 2:1 ratio - equirectangular photo.

Virtual Tour Profit

If you view this 360° photo flat on a screen, it will have a wave-like shape. This is how it is represented in a 2D or "still" type of environment. When a 360° photo is imported into virtual tour software, it centralizes the viewer, so when you look at the photo on a screen, it's like you're standing in the center of the room and looking around. With virtual tours created on CloudPano, the viewer can click a button on their mobile device that activates a "motion viewer" option. This allows the viewer to look in different directions by simply moving their phone – which feels very realistic and consumers love it. It's an interactive experience that's unique to 360° virtual tour technology.

You can also view 360° virtual tours in VR (Virtual Reality) headsets for an even more immersive experience. Even though the majority of people don't have access to a VR headset, there is increasing popularity. One day in the future there will be a VR set up in every household.

Viewing 360° virtual tours is not quite a video and not quite a still image – it's a new media, a new channel to view spaces.

The viewer gets to interact with the space – they can click where they want to go, tap a hotspot to go to the next room, look up at the ceiling, look down on the floor, look left, and look right. They can choose to view what's important to them, just as if they were physically in the real space. It gives the user a sense of control, which stimulates the entire experience. It's an interactive selling and marketing environment.

Virtual Tour Profit

Another powerful aspect is that you can customize the virtual tour. You can tell a story, add information spots, link to videos, and even allow the viewer to shop from inside the 360° virtual tour. Including these elements is really simple to do with tools like CloudPano. As you get more advanced, you can add additional elements such as video chat. That allows a seller to actually have a live conversation as the consumer is taking their tour – this creates a powerful virtual sales environment.

WHY IS 360° A POWERFUL SELLING TOOL?

360° virtual tours are exceptionally effective selling tools. Look at some of these statistics. Make notes of these;they're great statistics to quote for your own sales pitch!

- Customers aged 18 to 34 are 130% more likely to book a hotel room if there is a virtual tour.
- 50% of adult users on the internet rely on virtual tours in their research and decision-making process.
- Customers spend 5 to 10 times more on websites with virtual tours.
- 67% of people want more businesses to offer virtual tours.
- There are more than 5 million visits daily on worldwide virtual tours.
- Virtual tours increase a business listing's interest by two-fold.

Virtual Tour Profit

WHAT PROBLEM DOES 360° SOLVE?

The real estate industry has adopted 360° virtual tours for a good while. Regarding utilization of this technology, real estate is the leader.

An industry survey in 2020 showed that real estate listings with a virtual home tour get 87% more views! A large amount of real estate transactions are done with clients that are in a far away location and are unable to physically view the property. This creates a difficult obstacle in convincing clients to spend a large sum of money, as clients can feel uncomfortable about whether they are seeing everything needed. A 360° virtual tour allows the real estate agent to show the property with full transparency, and the client can feel more confident knowing that nothing has been hidden from sight. They can view the entire property as they wish.

Also, for the small business owner, it gives massive credibility to potential clients and customers. If your physical business is a beautiful space that you've worked hard to create, and you have an "interior fit out" that can shine when somebody sees the inside, showing off the interior of your space can build massive rapport with potential prospects.

Let's look at another example: If you are an auto dealer and you're trying to sell more cars, taking a photo of the interior of your vehicle in a traditional way is actually quite cumbersome. It's difficult to do. The interior is where someone spends most of their time in a car, so consumers will look at this with deep concern. But it's hard to display or share effectively with still photos. With a 360° environment, the virtual tour becomes an easy and effective selling tool for the auto market

WHAT NICHES ARE ADOPTING 360° VIRTUAL TOURS NOW?

One of the great things about starting a virtual tour business is that you have a very broad customer base – and it will only increase in size. There are many niches and industries that have adopted the power of 360° tours. And with the increasing popularity of 360° tours within those niches, competition will put pressure on all businesses to keep up with the trend or face losing market share. Here are a few examples of niches that are strong markets for 360° virtual tours:

Nursing/Retirement Homes

Nursing/Retirement homes have exploded since baby boomers are now increasing exponentially into retirement. With that, the competition is fierce to on-board and take more leads on those who are retiring into these nursing homes and retirement facilities. These types of facilities typically have very big budgets and are always looking to expand and grow their marketing. We have a user who sold a $5,000 virtual tour to a retirement facility, and he has plans to sell throughout his entire Wisconsin state if he's successful. There's about 900+ service providers within that niche. If he gets just 10% of that niche, it could generate $500,000 in revenue for him and his partner.

Construction Contractors

Virtual tours are also utilized in the construction world. There's phases to every project, especially large buildings, and different contractors or subcontractors come in to perform those specific tasks or trades. Contractors need to document and be able to prove that they did all the steps correctly. This ensures they are happy, and it creates an "insurance policy" for that general contractor. This market is huge and we already see providers tapping into it.

Real Estate

As mentioned previously, 360° virtual tours are huge in the real estate industry. That means that it can be saturated with providers and therefore real estate companies expect low prices, as well as a full service with still photography and traditional video. However, the real estate market provides a large volume of work, and it's never ending. So if this is the niche you want to go after, the game would be low margin, high volume work.

Virtual Tour Profit

Multi-Family Apartments

Some of our most successful providers are selling to multifamily and apartment building property managers. These budgets always recycle each year, and virtual tours are known to fill up more leases and help the marketing for large properties.

E-commerce

Virtual tours are taking a huge increase in the e-commerce world. 360° Virtual tours are being used to make physical brick and mortar stores into online platforms. A recent example is the luxury fashion brand, Ralph Lauren, who created a 360° virtual tour of their physical store. Links were attached to each item, allowing users to add them to their shopping cart.

Universities / Colleges

Virtual tours are heavily utilized to market universities and colleges. Walk-through tours of campuses are common and a big selling point for universities. In a recent conversation I had with the University of Alabama, they explained that their facilities do the selling for them, but they're losing that option as more students don't take physical tours and the excitement of being there is now going to have to be shifted to the virtual selling environment. We saw a CloudPano user sign up a local community college for $8,500, plus an ongoing monthly subscription of $250 per month. The initial job took him just 8 hours and the contract's two-year value was $14,500.

HOW DO CUSTOMERS BENEFIT FROM 360° VIRTUAL TOURS?

360° virtual tours have many powerful and convincing sales points, making them a pleasure to discuss with potential clients. In addition to the impressive statistics mentioned above, 360° virtual tours can positively affect the Google ranking of a client's website! Because customers spend a considerably longer time on websites that have 360° virtual tours, Google's ranking algorithm picks this up and ranks that web page higher in its search results. Also, Google Street View allows virtual tours to be added to a business owner's Google Maps listing. This lets people view inside a business when searching in your area on Google Maps. It's a highly effective marketing tool.

HOW TO CREATE A 360° VIRTUAL TOUR WITH NO EXPERIENCE

You'll need to start by getting a 360° camera (or if you are an experienced photographer, purchase a fisheye lens). There are many brands, and upcoming tech changes all the time. Every few months a new camera will "launch". However, a quick Google search will tell you everything you need to know about the latest options. If a 360° camera is out of your price bracket, there are also apps for your smartphone that allow you to create 360° photos from your phone's camera! Search the app store for CloudPano.

Once you have your camera, place it on a monopod in the center of the space and set a timer so you have time to exit the room. This way you can ensure you are not captured in the photo. Once you've taken the photo, transfer it to your computer and double check to see if it has been stitched together correctly.

There are settings and optimization you can implement to pull out the best colors of every photo. If you arebrand new, I recommend the "Auto HDR" inside your camera. This setting will help you move fast and start making virtual tours.

Then find yourself a professional photo editor to take your files and turn them into magic. When you find a photo editor, work alongside them to determine the best file types and workflows to make sure each project goes smoothly.

Next, upload the 360° images into the online virtual tour software CloudPano, and the creation should be easy and intuitive, even as a total beginner. You can do a number of things to your 360° environment such as connecting rooms and adding information spots. If you like, you can choose from different "themes", which are overall design templates that change the look of your design.

Once you're happy, click the "publish" button and you're all set to go! The whole process should take no more than a few minutes.

For creating a full professional experience, there's a big advantage in "private labeling". This is using your own customized URL for your business. CloudPano offers these options to people that upgrade to a Pro Plus membership for a small monthly fee.

What you can customize

You can customize a variety of features in your virtual tour experience. Here is what to expect as you dig into the software.

- The name and contact details of your client
- The overall design such as branding, colors, adding a logo, what images you want to use and where you use them, and the design of your icons
- You can customize the order of the photos where you're looking whenever you click onto a room (this is called Initial View)
- You can create natural movement navigation that keeps track of where you're located in the photo. You create these by just setting up a simple North point on each photo
- You can add 2D floor plans that can be used as a navigation map.

Some other advanced features that CloudPano offers include:

- You can turn on lead generation, which captures leads and sends them over to your clients.
- You can add password protection.
- You can connect Google Analytics to track your products usage.
- You can add a video call feature where your client can talk to the customer as they are interacting with the 360° virtual tour.

Virtual Tour Profit

Adding all of these features to an experience creates large enterprise value, especially with clients that have high-ticket items and each sale is super profitable. You can charge accordingly for adding these extra features.

GETTING YOUR FIRST SALE

One of the great advantages of starting a 360° virtual tour business is that you can start to sell (preselling) before having to invest in equipment or invest your time becoming an expert. When you sign up with CloudPano you'll have access to a number of demos as examples. You can clone demos and move them to your account.

Once you have a niche in mind and you are ready to approach, you can share these demos with them as an example to help explain the look and feel of a virtual tour. This saves you from spending time working for free within a niche. This will help you validate first and confirm you have a "market to message match."

Now let's dig into some foundations and truths that will direct your business as you build out an organization that scales.

In summary, to get moving quickly you can use a CloudPano demo to presell your first client. Once they agree to a price, you can invest in a camera (preferably a 360° camera), a monopod (your camera stand) and CloudPano.com Pro Plus membership (your 360° virtual tour software).

CHAPTER 2

Foundations – The insider truth of every transaction

How to find the pain.

Here's the truth. You do not need expertise to be an entrepreneur. You do not need an incredible new idea to be successful as an entrepreneur.

Really…

Ideas are free. Everyone has a great "idea."

Know someone who has lots of good ideas but never takes action? We all have that friend.

YOU DON'T NEED IDEAS

In this chapter I am going to teach you how to take a great idea and work backgrounds from a **need**. Yes, ideas are great and being creative as an entrepreneur has value. But sometimes our ideas keep us stuck - we don't know if anyone really wants our thing. So I want you to take your *great* ideas and put them on hold. Put your ideas on the metaphorical shelf - for this chapter.

Sure there are famous entrepreneurs that start with world-changing ideas and see them through to riches. But the majority of successful entrepreneurs find their success in markets that are already well established. Smart entrepreneurs find lucrative markets first, learn what's important to that market (finds buyers first), bring value, compete, and win.

To provide virtual tours as a service you do not need to become an "expert" at 360° photography before you can start your VR agency. You need to be an expert at listening to customers and building relationships.

YOU DON'T NEED TO BE AN EXPERT

Every week I see brand new virtual tour entrepreneurs get their first sale and start their journey - with **zero experience**.

If you know how to create a 360° virtual tour and all of your clients do not understand the creation process… congratulations, you're *the* expert! Even if learning the process only took you one afternoon, from start to finish, to figure out all the components and the steps.

Your comprehension time is irrelevant.

What makes you an expert is knowing how to do something that benefits your client and helps them solve a pain or reach a goal.

Your experience in a service is less important to the end client. What matters most? **Results**.

Let's dig into this mindset and help guide you as you get started in this business.

NO PAIN NO GAIN

You do not have to become the world's best 360° virtual tour provider or digital marketing expert to provide value to your clients. At the end of the day, your clients only care about one thing: They want to solve a problem.

This truth is at the core of entrepreneurship. Business is all about solving problems and making transactions. Just think about that for a moment. Every business transaction is really about a client having a problem and a person or business providing a solution for a fee. Some entrepreneurs have brilliant ideas, some have exceptional expertise, but when it comes down to it, success is about finding a problem that needs a solution.

So, your number **one** <u>most important</u> skill as an entrepreneur is the ability to find painful problems. Clients want to pay money to have the painful problems solved. This will always be true. As long as businesses have problems and pain, there will be a market for you to fill and money to be made.

My point is this, don't get stuck on the idea that being an "expert" or having the best idea will determine your success in your virtual tour business.

Instead, you need to be obsessed with finding pain. And the more specific the pain, the better.

HOW TO FIND THE PAIN

How do you find the pain? You need to be able to find their pain because pain is where the gold is hidden.

Every business owner has desires, they have goals and they have objectives. They also have roadblocks - things they have to do. Painful activities and needs that arise as they go about pursuing their goal. Whether they find themselves repeating painful tedious tasks or they need a solid process to acquire leads-and-sales. There is pain everywhere…

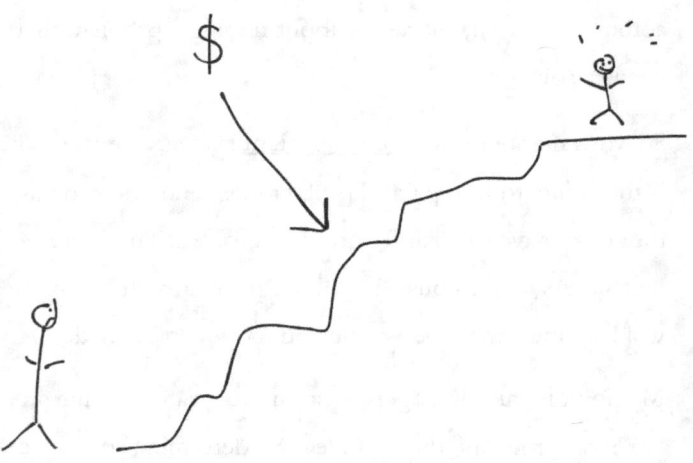

It's within these roadblocks and within these pains that the transactions are waiting for you. And if you get great at digging up pain and putting it on the table and discussing it, valuable transactions will naturally take place.

In the lifecycle of a sale, pain discovery must come first. Because when you present, pitch, and close a client, you must assign your service to an existing need. Otherwise, your client's investment won't make **logical** sense, and you won't make a sale.

Yes, 360° virtual tours are incredible tech. And yes, there are situations where the technology is so unique that it sells itself. But in the majority of transactions, the justification for the service is based on a specific need. You need clarity on what problem you are solving within your niche.

How do you determine this? Easy, you ask the niche to tell you.

For example: "What are your goals right now?" and "What is painful that's keeping you from reaching that goal?"

The more you speak to a prospective client, the more they will reveal what is really important to them and **why**.

When you discover a pain and lock into how you can help relieve it, your value will be clear and prospects' decisions become binary.

Which means you bring your prospective client to a state where they are asking a yes or no question. "Will <service/product> relieve or remove <pain> and be worth <price>?" If their answer is yes, then a transaction will move forward.

Now there are always market conditions that apply, but in general this is the last question you must answer before you make a sale. Notice that it's impossible to fill in this sentence without a valuable pain or problem? It's very important to establish this first (it's worth repeating).

Plus, if you can find a need inside a specific niche and you can solve it repeatedly, you can scale within that niche. But more on that later...

This process (finding pain first) applies to all types of services you can sell, not just 360° virtual tours. It's a repeatable process in sales psychology.

Before you begin selling any product or service to someone, you must understand two things:

1. Their current state
2. Their desire state

When you speak to any business owner, they will always be in their current state and will always have a desired state they want to achieve. If they knew exactly how to get to their desired state, they would already be there, right? So, it's your job to uncover what they need to achieve that desired state. If you can do that and offer a solution - how to fill the gap between the two states - you'll win every time.

Stick with me as I paint a picture:

Imagine you are in the middle of a Sunday lunch at home and

there is a knock on your door. You open it and there is an old-fashioned door-to-door salesman with a friendly smile. He's selling a set of encyclopedias. In the background your two children, aged 5 and 8, are running around the house screaming and you can't quiet them down. All you want to do is have a Sunday rest after lunch, but you have a splitting headache. Now with all the commotion going on, the last thing you want to hear about are the amazing features of this encyclopedia set. It's literally the last thing you feel like hearing in the world, even though the salesman has a perfect pitch lined up.

Here's what he might say:

"Hi there, I am selling these incredible encyclopedias. The full set is only $150 which is a discounted price just for today. They are excellent for your kid's education and they are beautifully leather bound with very good quality paper…"

Your lunch is getting cold, the kids are screaming and you have a headache. This conversation will end quickly.

But here's what a dialogue might sound like if the salesman understood the psychology of selling:

"Whoa, the joys of kids, right? I've got three myself, I love them with all my heart, but when it comes to Sunday afternoon I just wish they would be as quiet as mice."

"Ha! You understand…I guess it's all part of being a parent."

"Totally, but it's such an amazing experience being a dad that I'd never trade it for a peaceful Sunday."

"I hear you, I feel that way too. But I sure could do with a break every now and then, you know?"

"Maybe the universe had a hand in placing me at your door at 1:42pm on this Sunday! I've actually got a way to get rid of your headache AND make your kids happy every Sunday."

"You do? Not sure I believe that's possible but tell me, I'll do anything to make that happen!"

"What I do every Sunday with my kids is that after lunch, we have what I call 'Magic Hour'. For an hour, my three kids, myself and my wife, sit on the bed and look through these encyclopedias. Each of my kids has a turn at picking a random page and then I read to them. The kids love it. They get to learn something new about the world, and they get to ask lots of questions. There are also really amazing pictures. And afterwards they are usually sleepy and we all have a midday nap."

"That actually sounds like such a wonderful idea!"

Now you're fully engaged and ready to make a transaction. The truth is that the salesman doesn't even need to explain all the amazing features. He's already found your problem and offered you a solution. Through a short conversation he has identified your current state (stressed, headache) and identified your desired state (peace, quiet). He's also pinpointed what is of biggest value to you (happy children, being a good dad). And that's what a sale is all about!

I find this little story useful to keep in my mind when I pitch to a new client. Here's how it translates:

The "father" is the business owner. He has many stresses going on in the background. The "kids" that are giving him a headache could be any number of things from cash flow issues to accounting problems, staff difficulties to a flat tire on the delivery van. They may seem calm and composed but without a doubt, every business owner in the world is juggling many stresses all the time. Unless they have contacted you directly because they are considering which is the best virtual tour provider to go with, the last thing they will be in the mood for is to hear about all your great features. Talk about their problems and they'll be happy to share because that's what's on their mind.

PAIN-FINDING FRAMEWORK

Let's go through a pain finding framework to give more handles on this concept so you can use it in your next sales conversation. Each sales pitch should be unique, based on the personality of the client you are pitching. For example, if they are fun and relaxed, you should use simpler words, perhaps make a few jokes and have relaxed body language. If they are very serious and corporate-like, you should keep your sentences short and to the point to show efficiency and professionalism. But as a framework, here are 5 questions that you should ask to reveal the pain point and the value to solving that pain:

1. What is your most clear and present problem with _____?
2. How do you go about solving that problem right now?
3. What happens if you don't solve it?
4. What would your dream solution be or if you could wave a magic wand and everything was perfect? How would it look and feel?
5. Would that be worth paying for? If so, how much?

Now we'll go into the details of each one.

1. What is your most clear and present problem with _____?

In most cases you'll be asking about marketing, although it may also be sales, converting leads etc. This gets them thinking about what their problems are, and the first ones they mention will likely be the ones that are bugging them the most.

e.g. My sales aren't growing and I can't get more people to walk through the door

2. **How do you go about solving that problem right now?**
   Since they've noted this as a 'problem' area, whatever solutions they have currently put in place will not be working. It's a useful question because it will highlight their current ineffective strategies.

   e.g. we've put a sign up front and run some specials

   It can be a good idea to throw in an extra question at this point which is "**how is that working for you?**". This will bring their frustration into attention.

   e.g. we've spent so much money on these things and they haven't really changed anything at all

3. **What happens if you don't solve it?**
   What happens if they don't get those 10 extra sales per week or those extra 5 leads? How will it affect them in reality? The answer will get them thinking how important it is to prioritize this pain point and find a solution urgently.

   e.g. I'll have to close the business, I won't be able to take a salary that month etc.

4. **What would your dream solution be or if you could wave a magic wand and everything was perfect? How would it look and feel?**
   This prompts the client to think about how much better their world would be if they could find an effective solution.
   e.g. I would be so happy if we could get 10 new clients a month. That would change everything and we could be making a healthy profit. I'd be much more relaxed.

Now having asked these 4 questions, you've gotten to a place where your client has revealed their current state and their desired state. By getting them to speak the words out loud, you've also gotten them to emotionally connect to the pain point in this moment. Right now, they've forgotten about all of their many other problems and you have their full attention on the problem that you are about to solve for them.

5. **What would it be worth paying for? If so, how much?**
   At this point you are going to reveal something financial, a price point. What value does the business owner place on fixing this solution? How much does a solution mean to them?
   e.g. I've already spent $500 but nothing is working. If I could actually get this properly sorted out, I would spend up to $800 now. But if it really works then I'd be happy to spend another $250 every month.

[Reference: Start From Zero by Dane Maxwell]

At this point you can now present your solution and create

an offer for them. This could be your 360° virtual tour product and/or any number of services that you offer. One of the great things about virtual tours is that they can fit into so many different models that you can use as an entrepreneur. If you offer marketing services, run ads, are a lead generation expert, a photographer, videographer, graphic designer, or web designer, 360° virtual tours can be added neatly within all kinds of packages and business models.

360° virtual tours present a great perceived value. When a client invests in advertising, it's an abstract "hole" that money disappears into. But virtual tours are visual. The psychology of a client is that being able to actually see something that they are paying for makes them more satisfied that they are getting value. It's also more powerful than simply receiving a set of photos from a photographer because it is interactive and has intrinsic marketing value. It sits in a happy middle between a product and a service, and your client will see this as money well spent. This really helps you as you go about getting referrals from your current clients.

REVERSE ENGINEER YOUR OFFER

You will need to reverse engineer an offer. You now know what's important to your client and where they want to be, and this is the first piece of vital information. At first you may find yourself attaching prices to services that you don't really know their viability. That's totally OK, you have to start somewhere, and it's all part of the journey of being an entrepreneur.

A key piece of information is to determine the annual value that one customer equates to for their business. Once you know the pain and you know the degree of pain that you're trying to solve for your client, as well as the value of your solution by solving that pain, it is now possible to determine the equitable value of acquiring one customer per month for that client. This helps you lay the foundation of ROI (Return on Investment) based selling. Simply put, the principles of ROI based selling are that for every $x they spend with you, they make $x in revenue.

This means that your service is quantifiable, and nothing sounds more beautiful to a business owner than "quantifiable". There are many ways to calculate ROI and they can get rather complex. But to start, here is the simplest and most common ROI formula:

You take the sales growth from that business or product line, subtract the marketing costs, and then divide by the marketing cost.

Virtual Tour Profit

(Sales Growth - Your Cost) / Your Cost = ROI

Here is an example:

Your client owns an apartment complex and they are selling units at a price of $100,000 per unit.

On average they are selling 1 unit every 2 months (6 per year). With your 360° virtual tour service, you can increase their sales to 1 unit every month (12 per year)

They were earning $600,000 per year

With your service they will earn $1,200,000

That means a sales growth (the difference) of $600,000

For all your marketing services you charge them $2000 a month ($24,000 a year)

Now, putting this into the above calculation:

($600,000 - $24,000) / $24,000 = 2400% ROI per annum

Having a good ROI percentage to show is the strongest argument you can make in your sales pitch. At first you can base your ROI on an estimate, but once you get a contract and have a chance to prove yourself, if you can show real and consistent ROI then you are guaranteed ongoing work. After all, if the client is making more money each time they invest with you, what could be better!

IT ALL COMES DOWN TO DOLLARS AND CENTS

There are several differences between the psychology of an "artist" and a "business owner". Both are completely valid, neither is more correct than the other, but it should be taken into account in your sales strategy. An artist will typically place a high value on the quality and uniqueness of the product itself. If you are an artistic or creative person, you may feel the urge to focus your sales pitch on just how great your photography looks, how strong the visuals are, how much better the technical specifications of your camera's resolution are, etc. This may be a reasonable strategy if your client understands the tool too. But in most cases a business owner is focused entirely on the bottom line - the dollars and cents. They want to spend x amount of money and want to make x amount of money. They want to make a good investment decision. The effectiveness of your product in turning marketing spend into actual cash. This should be your main focus.

KNOWING YOUR WORTH

Understanding the monetary value of the growth you create helps you justify your pricing. If you can bring in $50,000 worth of revenue and are charging $5,000 for the service, that's very reasonable. Always remember to see your product as something that helps generate money. What you are selling is an asset. And your fee should always be seen as relative to the income it will produce.

For example (a silly one, but stick with me!), if you are selling a goose you might ask for $100 and the client might say "hmm...my budget is half of that. I don't think I'll go for it today." If you present the client with the same goose but raise the price to $1,000 and explain that it lays a golden egg once a week that's worth $500, things look quite different! Who wouldn't spend $1,000 if it means you make your money back plus a healthy profit? Suddenly $1000 seems like an incredible price. It's all relative.

Therefore, if you know that your client makes a big profit on each sale, you can justify a high price. Conversely if your client makes only a small margin on each client you bring in, you'll adjust your offering accordingly. At the end of the day, your service needs to make sound investment sense.

A general rule of thumb is a good price is 10% of the value created. This presents an easy ROI justification to any business owner.

Of course, in the real world there are other forces to be considered, such as competition. If your niche is oversaturated, and your local competitors are aggressive in their pricing, or your targeted industry is going through a low period, this will change your pricing strategy.

Be willing to customize offers based on the response and reaction of your clients. As I always say – "whatever it takes to get your foot in the door." Your first transaction with a client is the most important. Even if it is limited to a small job or is not at a fee that excites you, there is huge value in being allowed the opportunity to build a relationship. Your first jobs are invaluable. Your first jobs allow you to:

- Prove your product's results to the client
- Build a case study to show to future clients
- Gain experience in your skills
- Develop an on-going relationship with your client
- Potentially gain referrals

These points are each worth money. So even if your goal is to make big money, start off humble and focus on closing those early deals. Once you've built trust, shown real results, and learnt your skills through trial-and-error, you'll be set on course for success!

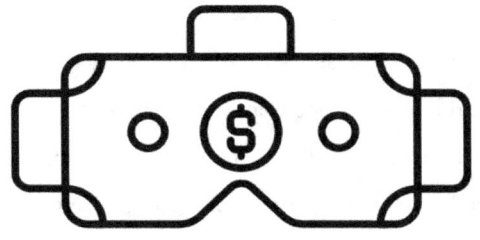

CHAPTER 3

The VR Digital Media Business Model

The multiple ways to monetize a virtual tour business

When putting together your digital marketing and VR business, it's **vital** to position yourself as a digital media company who provides solutions. You need to establish your business as a "problem solving machine." The more specific you can be within your niche, the better response you will receive from your marketing. This is called "market to message match".

For example, if your business is titled "360° VR Wizard" and your subtitle says "We create 360° virtual tours for everyone!" It's likely you will NOT resonate with your target niche. But if your company name contains "Media" or "Services" you will be able to create marketing language that resonates with your niche. For example: "Calhoon Media specializes in multi-family real estate digital media services that fill up leases and increases occupancy for property managers and real estate investors." If I am a property manager or an investor, I will pick up the phone and *call this company*. Because it's speaking directly to me. This messaging *resonates* with property managers and investors. The more you *resonate*, the better response you will receive.

The most powerful way to attract your niche is to demonstrate and share success stories from your previous clients. We call these "case studies." It's a well-established marketing method to show **proof** that you can help your future clients achieve their goals and objectives. This requires previous success. So, if you are brand new, this must be your initial goal. When you are starting to acquire clients, and "breaking into" a niche, you can cut deals in exchange for testimonials and case study documentation. My favorite way to document customer success is to interview them and ask them general questions about their story. Then record the call and use it as your first case study. Market your previous success and you can break into any niche you target.

As I am writing this chapter, I got this email…

Virtual Tour Profit

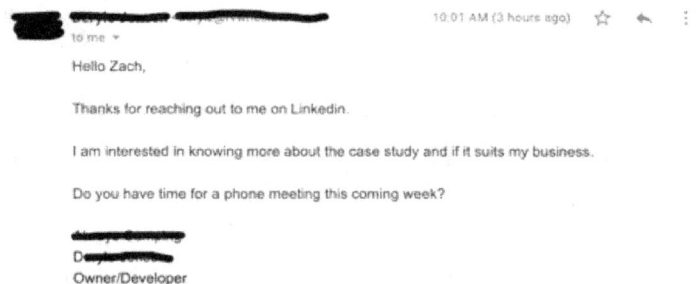

[I marked out his information from this image to protect his privacy]

When you start to publish your niche specific success, clients start to **come to you**. Wondering where to start? Start with getting clients their desired results, then market those results like crazy. I will cover more on this topic later in this book.

WAYS TO MONETIZE YOUR VR BUSINESS

When you get a new client, you get an opportunity to build a business *relationship*. A business relationship means you can offer different services on an ongoing basis. The smart entrepreneur takes full advantage of this!

I am about to share some services that you can provide your clients. These offers easily tie into your business model. Most of these services are not brand-new innovative offers. But that's fine! What makes your business unique is that **you** are the one to provide the results. Your goal is to become the trusted "go-to" provider. If your clients like you and trust you (because you consistently get the job done), then you'll get consistent calls when new needs arise. Plus you will get natural referrals inside business owner networks. Remember that the best marketing is word-of-month. Be the provider that everyone is talking about!

Layer on offers – Increase Customer Lifetime Value

<u>Hosting and Maintenance</u> – Charge Monthly Recurring Fees

In addition to the creation of the virtual tour asset – going on location and shooting the 360° virtual tour – a powerful offer is "Hosting & Maintenance". Since you are hosting the tour by sending a link to the client, you are delivering an asset that lives online and can be updated and upgraded. Because this deliverable can change post setup, you can continually deliver value and charge monthly hosting fees. Therefore, you gain a consistent and ongoing income stream. To justify this is simple. You are hosting the tour on a special server and you will maintain and update anything inside the tour throughout the year. If you are thinking "Zach, I don't want to always be changing things inside the tour for them…" Don't worry. Set the expectation that you will always be here to help for reasonable changes. If they start to send you massive requests, send them a bill to get started.

Virtual Tour Profit

Additional Features – Create "Advanced" Tours

Using software such as CloudPano, there are a wide variety of extra features that can be added to your virtual tour. For example, you can add buttons with further text information, capturing leads and including a live video chat feature. These extra add-ons are, in most cases, very desirable features to clients, as they further help their sales process to be more efficient. You can charge an additional fee for adding each feature. What's great is these features can be added in a matter of seconds, so there is little extra work for you. These extra items can be sold as a package or itemized out individually. Capturing leads through CloudPano means that with a click of a button, your client can receive leads automatically inside the tour. We call this the "Lead Generation" feature. If a viewer of the tour wants more information, they add in their details and CloudPano will send over those details to your client (automatically). This creates consistent value for your clients and justifies a consistent fee (which they pay you each month).

This is a popular approach because it aligns with your client's sales goals. *Every* client wants more leads, *every* client wants more sales! So, if your pricing strategy is a higher ticket offer, including lead generation, then you can justify the higher price based on the sales goals of your client.

<u>Selling Seats On CloudPano Live</u>

You can sell "seats" to CloudPano Live. CloudPano Live allows your clients and their prospects to have a live video chat inside a 360° environment. Inside this selling environment you can pass back and forth control and even draw on the 360° space. CloudPano lets you add "hosts" who have protected, controlled access to live video chat, which is available to your clients. Plus, you don't have to be present for this access. Your clients can jump into these 360° calls anytime. This can be a very important part of your sales package when you're selling a virtual tour. You're aligning with the sales team's needs and goals. If a sales team has several members, there is a fantastic opportunity for compounding monthly revenue, as you can charge a fee per seat. This ongoing revenue stream is passive income – after selling the product, it does not require any further work from you, other than sending that invoice!

Let's take a look at a hypothetical example where selling seats on CloudPano live can be highly effective.

Virtual Tour Profit

Custom home builders have a sales team, and if you sell virtual tours to them, they probably have a mixture of homes that are for sale right now - some of the product is already built and some of their product is homes that they are trying to sell before they build them. So a sales team can use a 360° virtual tour of their 3D rendering model and hop into a live call to walk their customer through the tour. Quickly, they have an entire environment where they're selling their inventory and it's super efficient for them. If you white label your tours on CloudPano, you can customize the experience for your clients and keep your brand on the tour link.

Selling Floor Plans To Clients

Also, you can create floor plans for clients, with CloudPano's floor plan uploading tool. While floor plans are typically in a blueprint type environment, you can make them more clean and presentable for the customer by customizing them with CloudPano's easy-to-use editing tools. You can have 2D plans and also 3D style plans – plus you can add hotspots to the floor plan and help the user navigate throughout the tour. You can also have CloudPano build these Floor Plans for you from the 360° virtual tour. So if your client asked for a Floor Plan (and you have long left the location), it's no problem!

Just order a Floor Plan with the team at CloudPano. Charge the client and keep the margin.

Google Street View As A Service
--

One of the easiest ways to sell virtual tours is to discuss a well-known tech product, Google Maps. Google has been sending out cars to photograph 360° photos of streets and businesses for years. So, business owners are well aware of Google's Street View product. As business owners create listings on Google Maps (Google My Business) they are prompted with the option to add a "virtual tour" of the inside of their business. This creates a common awareness among the small business owners in your community. But there's a catch. To assign a Google Street View interior virtual tour to a Google My Business listing, you are required to use 360° photos. This added need for 360° photos is a hurdle for the business owner and an easy solution for the provider (you!). Plus, connecting a small business to Google Street View can boost their SEO and Google search rankings. This benefit could, in fact, be your lead-in product with which you can start your value-sales conversation. As you teach your clients about Google Maps, Street View, and Google My Business, you can build authority and rapport. You can make

Virtual Tour Profit

Google Street View an upsell or part of your core offering.

<u>Photography and Video</u>

Photography and videography are services that tie in very well with 360° virtual tour packages. In fact, it's a common and a natural request as a digital media pro! With today's camera technology, professional photography is more accessible than ever. Many virtual tour providers started in the photography space and are expanding their services. But the competition in photography is fierce, and this drives prices down. Plus, if you have a new generation smartphone, you can supplement photography with video and a gimbal. Many new smartphones shoot 4K video, which is a professional level quality. It pays to offer these services alongside your virtual tours.

Case Study: How Stephen Farrell turns a virtual tour customer into a $50K video client.

I got a call from Stephen who shared an inspiring story. He walked into a meeting with a health and wellness clinic to sell a 360° virtual tour. The director comes in and sits down in the meeting and looks Stephen in the face and says, "I have 10 minutes."

Virtual Tour Profit

So, Stephen looked at him and said…

"I take it you are a meat and potatoes kind of guy?"

Mr. director nods

"Well, I create 360° virtual tours and I create videos."

Mr. director says "well I would like a quote to create 50 videos, which includes all of our services we offer here." (It's a large clinic).

Stephen says "I can put that together for you, but to make sure these are high quality videos they will need to be at least $1,000 each. You don't want videos that cost less than that."

Director: "Ok send me a quote on paper and we can talk more."

Stephen agrees and leaves the meeting.

In this situation, Stephen walks into the meeting ready to sell the benefits of a virtual tour, and he leaves with a $50K video prospect.

That's the power of offering multiple services.

Website Design As A Service

Another great service to upsell is web design. This may sound complicated but it's not. All you need is access to a trusted developer who can output what you need. You can outsource the project quickly and even use templates or past project examples from your web developer (with permission of course!).

There's a great trend in the marketplace today for "landing pages". These are simple, one-page websites that potential customers will be directed to when they click on an online social media advertisement. A landing page introduces the consumer to your client's company and product or service and then has a "Call to Action" – which will prompt the prospect to book a meeting or fill out a form.

Lead Generation

You can also offer a more advanced (but still relatively simple to learn) service like Lead Generation. Here you'll set up a simple campaign via Facebook ads or Google PPC to create traffic for your client's landing page that captures the lead and sends them automatically to your client. You are buying advertising on your client's behalf, setting up the landing page (which you will also be designing for a fee) and you can then set up automation software that connects your client to their new leads. The power of this service is that it is *quantifiable*. After running an initial campaign, your client can see *exactly* what revenue was generated from what they spent on ads. If there is a positive ROI (Return on Investment) then you'll be guaranteed ongoing business. For example, if you can say "you spent $1000 and you made $3000", that's a clear value proposition to continue the service.

Database Set Up

Another upsell opportunity is to offer the service of setting up a database for your client. Every business needs a database – a regularly updated list of past clients and potential future clients that they can reach out to. Using online tools (Active Campaign, Aweber, Mailchimp etc.), you can set up a database fairly easily and charge your client a one-time fee. You can also set up auto-responders and white label the database for your client to add more value and charge a recurring fee to maintain this for them.

SETTING EXPECTATIONS

In time, with enough experience and enough contracts, you will indeed become a professional at one or more of these additional services. But don't let the lack of experience stop you from offering them as part of your package. As mentioned, many of these additional services are actually quite simple to set up or outsource. Business owners are busy with many different issues and want to focus on their core business. So in effect you're saying "focus on what *you* do best, and let *me* work on these things for you."

In business it's always best to be transparent and to set expectations with your clients. If you're new to one of the services, such as web design, say to them "I'm fairly new to this, but I do have some excellent templates I can use. They won't be fully customizable, but they'll do a great job." You can show them an example or two of what you can do so they understand the level of service that your experience can deliver.

Whatever services you plan to offer – whether it is web design, photography, video or any others – it's a good idea to first do a test run before you offer the service to a client. For example, if you want to offer photography, do a photo shoot of a property – your own home may be an easy place to start.

Once you have done this, you will have familiarized yourself with the process and also it will give you an example that you can show to your client. As another example, if you want to offer web design, create a website for a fictitious company – one that is relevant to your niche.

Some clients may have a big budget and want to hire the best in the business, but many clients will be perfectly happy with templates that you have prebuilt so they can move fast.

OUTSOURCING

Most of these add-on services can be outsourced! You'll easily be able to find plenty of freelancers locally and there are also many freelance websites where you can outsource work to. For services such as web design, logo creation or graphic design, you can outsource to a freelancer anywhere in the world! If you choose to go this route, you can add a margin on top of their fee and simply focus on the selling. There is a simple rule of thumb here: if it's digital, I can find someone to quote me a price and get it done quickly.

CREATING A VALUE LADDER

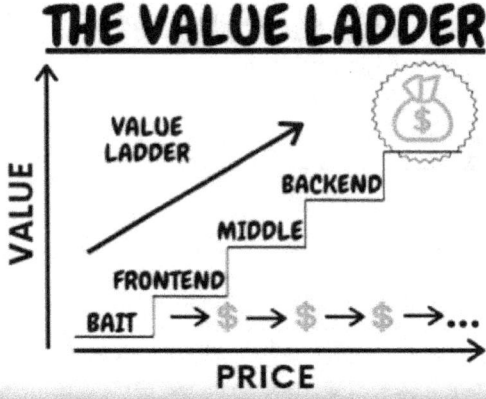

To visually see the offers you will be creating, I want you to build a "value ladder." This helps you see the potential offers you will create for clients. Creating a value ladder is to design a business that creates multiple offers that solve multiple problems for your clients. The exercise of designing a value ladder is to draw out your offers and make assumptions based on the price points and value. The more value you offer, the higher your price. The reason you want to draw out your offers, whether it's a lower ticket or higher ticket, is because it helps inform visually what offers you will be creating and mentioning whenever you're having a client conversation. Putting this down with pen and paper can help you visualize and understand your strategy, and it's something you can keep and refer to in the future. You can stick this on the wall next to your desk so it can remind you of your overarching strategy every day.

Free / Lowest Value Offer

When you are engineering a value ladder, your lowest value offers have the least touch points and physical requirements from you. This may be a "bait" type offer, and can even be something that you are offering for free. Sometimes offering one of your services at no charge or at a discount, especially a service that doesn't require much of your time, can create great customer value and the money can easily be made back on the items you do charge for. These offers can lead to an easy "yes" and an invaluable foot in the door. These low ticket / free items will go to the bottom of your value ladder.

Core Offer

Going up a rung in the ladder is your core offer. This is the "good stuff" – what you're known for, what you're good at, what you love to do. The core offer is often easy to digest and repeatable. Most of your clients want your core offer and don't need much time to think it over.

High Ticket Offer

Your Ascension offer or "High Ticket" offer is a robust offering that will make your client's life perfect and wonderful! It may require the highest amount of work from you, but that is why it is justified as being your high ticket offering. What you want is a good product mix – the kind that gets your clients to say "yes, yes, yes". In sales, that's what is called the "yes momentum" and it's a big deal in marketing because many of the clients that buy your core offer will likely want to pay you more for something else. Each time you get your client to say the word "yes", the following yes becomes easier and easier. Remember, your clients will have lots of needs and they are busy. Once you have them in a position where they like you and trust you, if you are offering to help solve more of their problems this will be music to their ears. It's a headache to have to go out and find a new person and go through the hassle of interviewing strangers and taking risks. You're already in front of them, they like you, so it's an easy decision for them to simply say "Hey, I like you, I trust you, it would be great if you could do these other things for me as well!".

PUTTING IT ALL TOGETHER

When you are engineering your offers and determining what you want to do and how you want to do it, start with your core offer. Know what you're good at and know the value. Consider carefully the price points you desire to achieve. Your core offer needs to **make sense** to the market. Your core offer is where your sales pitch will hang upon. In a way, think of it as the wall that holds your ladder up.

Then you're going to want to construct a high ticket offer, something that offers much more and increasing value is a turn key solution. Be bold with selling high-ticket items. If selling for higher prices is new to you, prepare to be surprised at how many clients will opt for your most expensive offer. I like to ask myself "what would Christmas look like in my business?" That's your price goal for your high ticket offer. It should be an "all the bells and whistles" offer, and when you pitch, it needs to be *available* – a slide in your deck, ready to be proudly shown off.

I have seen offers be price anchors. The goal of only making a core offer looks easier to swallow. Yet at times - the highest ticket offer gets the conversion (even unexpectedly).

CREATE YOUR BAIT

Then you want to go back to the bottom of your ladder and reverse engineer a lower ticket offer. These bait offers make it easy for the client to enter into your world, something that helps solve a simple pain or problem in exchange for an email or contact information. In the digital marketing world, this can be a program or some type of training.

For example, if your niche has a recurring question they continue to ask, make that a free guide or lead magnet on your website. Your goal is to get passive prospects to "raise their hand" when they reach your site. Ideally your introductory low-ticket offer is something that is *scalable* and digital.

Once you work out these elements, you'll have your value ladder ready and you can visualize the customer journey. This is key as you work out the customer story.

It's important to note that these offers will change over time. As you learn more about your niche, you will be able to see which offers are easy to sell, and which offers match with your client's needs. It's important to listen and test your offers to clients. As you have success, you will have clarity and a repeatable business model that's natural for your clients to continually say yes.

CHAPTER 4

Engineering Awareness: The Five Levels

The five levels of awareness and why it's vital to your selling process

Eugene Schwartz is highly regarded as a successful copywriter and he wrote multiple popular books about sales and marketing - his most famous book is called *Breakthrough Advertising*. This book is rare to find in a physical form. Last time I checked Amazon, you could grab a copy of the book for $400 (yep just 1 copy). A famous concept from this book is known as "Schwartz's 5 Levels of Awareness". I've found this an extremely effective tool to map out the customer journey and determine my exact messaging as I plan a marketing or sales message.

In essence, it's about identifying your customer's "Level of Awareness" quickly to inform your sales approach and next steps.

Here are the five levels and I'll go into each in detail in this chapter:

1. Unaware (I have no idea there is a problem)
2. Problem Aware (I've got a problem, is there a solution?)
3. Solution Aware (Solutions exist out there and I am looking for a fit)
4. Product aware (I know you and your product/service, but are you right for me?)
5. **Most Aware** (I know you, I love you, I want to buy and refer you to everyone I know!)

Understanding your customer's level of awareness allows you to craft your sales pitch in the most effective way. The goal of understanding these stages is to guide the customer to Level 5, which is "Most Aware" – the level at which they are fully aware of you and your offering and are ready to sign up! The end-goal principle is:

The more aware of your prospect, the more money they're willing to give you.

Pay careful attention to each step – this can revolutionize the way you structure your sales pitch, and it really simplifies the sales process.

Certain niches being exposed to 360° photography and VR are going to be completely new to the concept. Which is why you need to be careful throwing around words like virtual, VR, 360° etc. You'll quickly find your prospect's eyes glaze over and disengage. This is why **talking about the utility before we talk about the problem is always a bad idea.** Especially in a new industry where many clients are not familiar with this tech, it's so important to note their awareness level.

So let's jump in! Here are more in-depth explanations about each of the levels:

Level #1: UNAWARE

At this most basic of levels, your prospect is not aware of you and your business and is not aware of the problem. You know of the problem, but because the customer does not, it's not one of their pain points. As an example, Google Street View can be a great help for a local business to gain new leads. However, your prospect may not know much about Google Street View or may not even be aware that it's a useful sales tool.

At this level of "Unaware", you are typically cold-calling a new prospect, perhaps sending out an email. Imagine if you were to start your pitch by saying "I can help you with Google Street View by offering 360° photography and a virtual tour". Immediately, the prospect will be uninterested because they have many other things on their mind, and they're not looking for this solution. In fact, they don't even know what it is all about! You may think that business owners are always interested to learn about new things, but remember that a business owner is constantly bombarded with unsolicited sales pitches. Because they have limited time and stress, their first reaction is to ignore, unless something catches their *interest*.

At this level of awareness, you will need to explain why they SHOULD be aware. Compare these two different opening lines:

"We offer a professional Virtual 360° service and we have the best prices around!"

The prospect will ignore this because they are (most likely) unaware of a virtual 360° tour and they don't know why they would need one.

vs.

"Did you know that Google Street View is a powerful and inexpensive way to gain new leads?"

This will get the prospect's interest because you've now made them aware of something they didn't know. You haven't even mentioned your core business, which is VR 360° tours. You've started by simply making them aware of something that they hadn't thought of before, and you're hinting at a solution to a problem you know that every business owner has – how to get more leads!

Level #2: PROBLEM AWARE

At this level, the prospect knows they have a problem – they have a pain point – but they are not aware of a solution, and if you understand your niche, you will have identified their typical pain points. For example, in the real estate industry, agents are always looking for new listings. Acquiring new listings is often prioritized over the actual selling and marketing of their current properties. For a real estate agent, more listings mean more opportunities. I saw a great example of marketing at this "problem aware" stage. It was a website of a real estate photography team and on their home page, the headline was simply "Win More Listings!"

Here, instead of saying something like "I produce top-quality real estate photography", the photography team focused on immediately giving a solution to a problem that they **know** their potential customer is always thinking about and is seeking a solution for.

If you are still speaking to clients and trying to understand if they are problem aware, ask this question, "when you go to bed at night and lay your head on your pillow, what problem keeps bothering you." This will quickly get you the information you need.

Level #3: SOLUTION AWARE

At this level, the prospect is aware of both their problem and also what solutions exist. So for example, they know that they need to have their business on Google Street View and they know that the solution is to get a 360° Virtual Tour from a pro (like you). At this stage of selling, you're now past the need for educating, and your job is to present yourself as the best company for providing that solution.

Typically this type of lead is inbound. They are calling you because they are educated enough to start and shop around for solutions. You speak to these types of prospects differently than an outbound lead. You can ask questions about their project and quickly determine the scope and assign a service or product to their need.

Level #4: PRODUCT AWARE

At this level, the prospect is aware of you and your product. The question they have now is "are you right for me?" and your job is to convince them that you are! It's at this point that you can delve into the finer details of your service and your strengths. Showing past successes is one of the strongest sales approaches and will give the client confidence in your real-world results.

List all of your strongest case studies and results early and explain that you specialize in their industry/niche.

Here is an example of a sales point list for the "product aware" stage:

Virtual Tour Profit

<u>List Example 1 - Results Focused</u>

1. We've helped over 50 businesses in your niche to get more leads (tell a specific story).
2. The high quality of our 360° virtual tours get over 5,000 views per month (show examples).
3. We specialize in your industry/niche so we have a lot of experience with your market and we have learned (insert specific valuable point).

<u>List Example 2 - Offer Focused</u>

1. Our prices are very affordable and the return on investment is excellent.
2. We have a very quick turnaround so can get you up online within ten days.
3. We've just invested in the very latest camera equipment.
4. We can offer a wide range of other services as well and believe in building long-term connections (and we are willing to negotiate to get started in our business relationship).

Level #5: MOST AWARE

This is the final level – the jackpot! Here the client is aware of the problem, aware of the solution, aware of you and aware of why you are the right fit for them. They know you, buy from you and refer you to everyone they know.

When you close deals and get your customer to success, they have a bond with you. It's at this stage you can ask for referrals and reviews. You can literally send direct links to your review pages and let them give you a quick 5 stars. Think of your recent customers as your advocates. When they go to a party, you want them showing off your virtual tour to **everyone**.

PRACTICAL USAGE

Remember that at Levels 1 and 2, your sales strategy should focus on *educating*. Only once your client reaches Level 3 (Solution Aware), can you begin introducing your direct sales pitch and explain why you are the right person for them. If you are speaking face-to-face with a client, start your conversation with the lowest-level question, for example "Are you aware of Google Street View?" If they say "no" then you're at level one. If they say "yes" then you can continue the questions through the stages, for example "Are you aware of how to get your business on Google Street View?" "How are you using your Google My Business page currently?" etc.

You should keep these 5 stages in your mind when approaching any of your sales methods, whether it's cold-calling, emailing, writing blog posts, or advertising. Even if you're in a face-to-face meeting with a prospective client, try to ascertain as early and as quickly as possible where they are located on the "level of awareness" spectrum. This will help you in knowing how to adapt your sales pitch so you are effectively guiding them through each stage of awareness.

In Summary:

To discover your customers' awareness level, ask lots of questions and pin down where they are on this spectrum. Then ascend with them as quickly as possible by bringing value and educating.

If you are writing your marketing or email campaigns, always assume your reader knows nothing and is barely aware of their problem. When you write like you speak, and walk your prospects through the process slowly, you will create marketing that resonates.

CHAPTER 5

How to Charge High Ticket Prices For Your Virtual Tours

Charge More and Scale Your Enterprise

If you charge more money, your potential for scale dramatically increases. Virtual tours unlock high ticket transactions for a variety of reasons. Even a few of these big ticket clients each month can drastically improve the health of your business. The easiest way to charge a high ticket is to target customers who are <u>large entities with big problems</u>.

Custom virtual tours create massive enterprise value for large clients. When you sell a virtual tour as a virtual selling environment, it aligns with the sales team's goals, so when you have a client with a sales team, you're providing a marketing resource tool that they can use in their pitch and selling process – in effect you are a valuable part of their team.

When pricing high ticket custom virtual tours, you need to make sure they are robust with features – It doesn't matter that these features and customizations generally take little time to create and deliver to clients.

With virtual tour pricing between $3,000 to $10,000, you can hire and build an organization that can scale. For example, one of our CloudPano Pro Plus users, Mark Rutherford, sold a virtual tour to a township for $10,500, plus an annual subscription of $300 a year. Pro Plus member, Jordan Powers, sold to a community college for $8,500, plus a subscription for $250 a month. He's now building an organization and pays his commission to a sales rep, and when we last spoke, he was looking at hourly employees to do the photography itself. He explained in our Facebook group that it only took him eight hours of work to create the virtual tour for that client. If you do the quick math, that works out to approximately $1,812 an hour for just one client! Plus, in the community college niche, he can leverage that CloudPano tour to many other colleges as he goes out and sells locally in the Minnesota area. In fact, a few months after he sold this project, he sent another message where he sold a different client an $18,000 virtual tour. It's a great story!

Selling To Multi Location Customers

There are many other great success stories with CloudPano users, such as Heather Eakins, who sells 60+ apartment locations, 30 at a time, and just one contract works out to $100,000 in revenue. And she did it twice! She made sure to include subscriptions per unit, which she photographs for around $400 + $25/month per unit. Plus the full apartment amenities walk through for around $1,000. Her subscriptions work out to be around $33,000 a year (if they decide to have at least three units per location on the books).

Then there's Julie, a CloudPano Pro Plus user, who sold a 35 apartment complex contract in the Charlotte area, and Rick, who sold a 30 apartment complex project to property managers (then he sold a 12+ location nursing home contract on CloudPano soon after). What this shows is that you can charge higher ticket packages when you're photographing multiple locations. It makes sense to the client, because you're doing a lot of work, a lot of travel. The client's perception is that it takes a long time to create these virtual tours, even though we know creating a virtual tour on CloudPano is actually quite simple, fast, and fun!

With the deliverables being so robust, the personal customization, the ongoing maintenance as needed, and with the whole package being high in value, you can charge high ticket prices for this type of service. In addition, as we mentioned, the CloudPano Live service also aligns with your client's sales team, so this further warrants a high ticket price. Try your best to determine:

- How many salespeople does your client have?

- How much will they be utilizing the tool?

- What is the value of their clients?

- What is the equitable value we're going to be justifying for this price?

Also, remember that you can have a base price and then charge per photo above that base.

So, let's say your package includes a number of photos that you offer, perhaps 5 to 10 360° photos. But you know that location has a need of 40 or even 60 different areas that you're going to have to create 360° photos for. Then the client can have the option to increase the pricing by increasing the scope on their own. Your client then has the option to back into a higher ticket price as their appetite for featuring more locations increases over time.

Itemize The Steps – Justify The Price

Alternatively, you can just create one flat fee and itemize all the services, make your service look really complicated, and make sure they know all the value they're getting from hiring you, the professional service provider.

Front Load The Subscription

Another option is that you can take the subscription model and front load it to justify increasing your price. That could mean an annual subscription that's included in the project.

Or you can spread out those payments monthly and you can charge per seat to use special features. Lead generation or Cloud Pano Live are things that can help you create packages that make sense but are tied to R.O.I., and are thus justified with higher ticket type services.

Presenting Higher Ticket Prices

What's the best way to present higher ticket prices in a selling environment? Previously, we've discussed how you find the pain, understand the equitable value, and the ROI of using your service. But more importantly, when you bring someone through a presentation, whether it's short or it's a long deck that you walk someone through in a boardroom, **the price needs to come at the end**. People need to understand at the end of the sales presentation how you arrived at your price. You need to build up the expected results and build the value of the services. You do not want to present your pricing too early. Make sure you have a *clear* understanding of their pain and you have shown exactly how you are going to **crush it** for them.

If someone asks you for a price quickly in a sales conversation, the answer is always the same:

"It depends."

You need to ask them what they are trying to do? How large is the scope of a virtual tour? How many features are they going to want to utilize? How much customization do they want to add to that virtual tour? In addition, you need to ask yourself: How much time will that take me? How many resources will I have to use in order to create this in a professional manner and make it **world-class** and make sure the client **loves it**?

When you ask these questions, you start to piece an offer together alongside your client. This is how you close big ticket services.

When you compare this to still photography, you are more *commoditized* in the photo world. Everyone has a camera on their phone, everyone has the "ability" to take a picture, so that ability has commoditized the market, and it's very difficult to build a value for it. It's still possible, but more difficult in the current market. You can still charge high ticket prices to your clients for still photography if you follow the same framework, understand their pain, understand what they need, build up your expertise, show the *art* and *creativity* behind the quantitative virtual tour creation. There will always be a creative side to the 360° virtual tour service – harness that, use it. Art is often highly variable in the pricing environment. If someone can buy into your thesis in what you are showing, what you're going to create, they'll want to buy into your high-ticket prices.

YOUR THESIS

To sell to a client, you have a hypothesis that you will be betting on – either you know it is true because you've done it before, or it's what you think will be true because you are going to provide an output and solve your clients' pains and problems.

This is called a "thesis".

It's a long form content piece that helps you prove a clear point to your client of how your service is going to help them reach all their desires.

Your thesis tells the customer's journey - where they are now, where they're going to go, how they're going to get there, and what **transformation** they will experience by using you and buying from you. Every customer needs a transformation. The higher price bracket you are charging, the more revolutionary the transformation needs to be. This means you need to be able to articulate a transformation and articulate to your client who they will become by using your service, and how all their competitors will have *no chance* against them. When this is communicated clearly and the story is enticing, the price becomes a secondary thought.

Virtual Tour Profit

How do you communicate a thesis that is clear and compelling?

You can create a long blog post, explain your service, what you do, what transformation your clients go through.

You could create a video where you're sharing your screen, showing examples, showing what virtual tours do, showing off the features and the results you've already gotten for previous clients.

You can also do this over the phone in a simple conversation and just talk about who they'll become. You could do this on a Zoom call, a sales call, with a slide deck showing the steps you take your customers through and who they become and what results they should see by using your service.

This type of thesis framework is important when selling higher ticket items because your clients must buy into your thesis and believe it's true before they're willing to buy from you.

This means if prospects have any questions or doubts about your service, answer them **prior** to pitching them on price. If you answer all their questions, if you have knocked down every leg of the stool, if they believe your thesis and if they buy into your thesis logically and emotionally, they'll buy your price and make a transaction.

CHAPTER 6

How to Sell Recurring Subscriptions For Your Virtual Tours

Why it's more profitable and more fun

Selling subscriptions is your secret weapon to profit and equitable value. Subscriptions are important because you can create a portfolio of customers and create *future* cash flow a*nd* increase the equitable *value* of your business.

When you sell recurring revenue, you create predictable income. This makes your business much easier to run (and way more fun). You wake up to sales! This way you can avoid the natural ebb and flow of service based business income. With recurring revenue, you can literally count down the number of customers needed to cover your operating cost and create freedom in your business and **in your life**. It's the fastest way to relieve money stress and unlocks a new world of business for you.

Also, if you want to sell your business one day, you can easily **double or triple** the value of your business by having a portfolio of subscriptions. A business with active subscriptions is highly attractive to investors and business buyers because it creates predictable cash flow and established future revenue. The main driver of a business value is the **future** cash flow. Your historical performance can help you prove the demand and your business model, but it can't pay you in the future. The multiples on subscriptions are much higher than the multiples for service-based revenue. You can reverse engineer this by adjusting your business model to your advantage.

THE FUTURE VALUE OF YOUR BUSINESS

How to think long term…

Let's take a moment and look ahead (into the crystal ball of the future). Can we answer the question… What will my business be worth in 3 years?

Let's compare the value of your business without subscribers.

Virtual Tour Profit

If we're operating by the industry standard, at the end of your financial year, you'll take your gross revenue, subtract your expenses, and be left with your "net" revenue. A typical service business is valued by a multiple of 1.5x to 2.8x of your **net** annual cash flow (some markets vary even lower).

A back of the napkin business calculation would look like this:

Net revenue x multiple = Cash value of your business

For example, if you grossed $100,000 in a year and you subtract your operating expenses and what you paid yourself, and you are left with $15,000 in the bank at the end of the year. A business buyer may pay you $15,000 to $42,000 for your book of business and operations.

If you have a subscription portfolio, the net revenue is less important, it's the subscription revenue that's the main driver of your business value. What this means is that a business buyer is willing to pay you 4x to 8x times the revenue you bring in each and every year via subscriptions. So, if you think about valuing your business this way, every time you get a subscriber, just multiply that subscription per month by 12 (annualizing the revenue) and then assign a 4x to 8x multiple on top of it. And in some markets, you can get a 10x multiple on your subscription revenue!

A back of the napkin business calculation for subscription based businesses.

Net revenue + (Annual recurring revenue x multiple) = Cash value of your business

Let's use the same example above that you brought in 75K of gross revenue for the year but you also have 40 customers paying you $97 each month ($3,880/month). Even if your net revenue for the year is $0, but you have an annualized subscriber base of $46,560, you can tag a 6x multiple to that subscriber base and value your business at $279,360. The investor is happy here because he has a predictable revenue stream, and he can increase the value by adding more subscribers. Meanwhile, you are happy because you just sold your business for much more than $15,000. ☺

Now market forces are always at play, and at the end of the day, a business is worth what someone is willing to pay for it.

The point is clear – to increase your business value, make sure your business model includes subscriptions.

WHY YOU CAN CHARGE SUBSCRIPTIONS AS A VIRTUAL TOUR PROFESSIONAL

There's a big advantage with virtual tours over many other one-off services. The main reason you can charge a recurring fee is that the deliverable is **hosted**.

When you sell a virtual tour and mention the subscription, you want to use the words "hosting" and "maintenance", and subscription-type phrases. Attach the subscription number to an ROI at the end of the year, and folks will have no problem paying it.

When you get to the pricing conversation, you want to **lead with subscriptions**. Do not hide the fact that in your pricing there is a hosting and maintenance fee. When you mention it, immediately detail what the subscription covers.

For example, "we host the virtual tour for you, and we can update it anytime throughout the year. If you have any new products to feature or a new salesperson's email, we can swap it out and send that person the leads through the tour." And if you include CloudPano host seats (which I highly recommend) you will want to include these in the hosting mentioned.

Virtual Tour Profit

If you want to add more CloudPano host seats to your account, just reach out to the support staff and they can give you a bigger account so you can scale this offer to your clients.

THE FASTEST WAY TO SELL SUBSCRIPTIONS

The fastest way to sell subscriptions is to target customers who also charge subscriptions or that have high-volume sales and inventory needs.

We have many examples of CloudPano Pro Plus users successfully selling lucrative subscription models within commercial and multifamily real estate. Auto, boat, and RV dealers are also examples of ideal subscription clients, as they expect a lot of volume to move through their business. You could charge subscriptions per salesperson or per vehicle, or just per showroom floor.

Also, small business owners who sell subscriptions for things like fitness studios, bike studios etc., expect subscriptions or annual fees for any activities that they are paying for. They already get subscriptions from their customers, so they're calculating: is it worth it for the lifetime value of my customer? Will I make a few extra customers per month by adding this marketing into my rolodex?

Again, you want to keep repeating phrases like "hosting" and "maintenance" and build features in your subscription model. For example, on CloudPano we have a lead generation model. When you white label your Pro Plus tours, this sends leads to your clients. It happens automatically – requiring no further work from your side once it's set up and running. These leads are delivered from a private domain, so it comes through to your client as "360° Virtual Tour Lead".

With the virtual tour acting as a lead capture mechanism, it perfectly aligns with the number one priority of any client – **sales**. Clients, no matter what their industry, are constantly asking the questions "How can I get more leads?" "How can I get more sales?" "Have I increased revenue?" The CloudPano features, especially the Live Video chat, make selling easy and give the client consistent value. It simply makes sense, and the client will be happy to pay for it.

So how do we use the words "hosting" and "maintenance" in our pitch? It's simple! You can say "we're *hosting* this virtual tour on a server." You can explain that with ongoing *maintenance* you can come in and edit it at any time if their details change. Your secret is that CloudPano makes this extremely simple. You can open a tour into your dashboard and edit virtual tours, information spots, HTML elements in your videos, and customize as your client needs it.

What you have is an environment that allows you to upsell. If your client provides you with new content, great! You can add it into the tour and provide the customer experience. Or they may want to add more logos or custom videos inside the virtual tour. If they want to add more images to detail certain small aspects of their facility or of their inventory- well, great! "We'll come out there and provide those. And here's a quote for us to professionally photograph the items within that space." All of these things help justify the subscription fee. In addition, clients generally prefer spreading out their costs by opting for a subscription model. It helps them limit the amount of cash outlay for the month.

Case Study: How David Sold a Client For $300 Per Month (Plus $3,000 To Set Up)

David Groves jumped into a VTPS group call and shared his recent win. "I told them this, they can give me $1,500 upfront and another $1,500 when they get their next client. That's also when hosting starts." And I asked him his hosting fee… "$300 per month." Wow! I was kind of surprised, but he was able to get it easily because he was targeting a nursing home client that really needed virtual tours to sell more customers. The lesson here is this: you need to get creative with how you close the customer. In this case, 1 client easily covers the cost. So, David made the value prop simple, pay me when you get your first paying customer – the risk is zero. This is possible for you as well if you target the right customer and build a relationship with the decision maker.

IDEAS TO HELP YOU CLOSE

How can you present recurring fees to a client? You'll explain that you will be available anytime to edit, add to, or update this virtual tour. You'll host it for them, and you'll provide all these tools and resources consistently. And, of course, this additional service comes with a fee. You'll explain that you're providing a **partnership** type service – far beyond just providing photographs, you're providing a marketing suite and a partnership that will help them to get more customers. Music to any client's ears!

What we're illustrating here is that you should position yourself as a marketing agency – a VR digital agency with the technology and resources to help your client win. This is how you position yourself to charge subscriptions.

Now, how does this change the math of your business? Earlier in this chapter I shared the business value metrics that come alongside subscriptions. Now I want to show you the compounding cash flow changes that come with the subscription model.

Virtual Tour Profit

The Old Way vs The New Way

You go off and get 100 customers at $1100 each. That's worth $110,000, which is great, but as these are on-off payments, the ongoing value to your business is zero. In year one, it's worth $110,000, but in year three it's still worth that same amount. That's not a great value- for busting your tail to get those sales!

The New Way

The new way is to go get 100 customers PLUS subscriptions. Your set-up fee could be lower – perhaps instead of $1100 it's $750. But you charge a subscription of $97 a month.

So, here's what that means for each client:

Year 1: $1914 ($97 x 12 months + $750 set up fee)

Year 2: $1164 subscription fees

Year 3: $1164 subscription fees

The 3 year value for your 1 client acquisition is $4,242

So instead of 100 customers = $110,000 three year value (the old way)…

Acquire 100 customers PLUS a subscription, and your 3 year value is $424,200!

At almost 4x the value, it's clear to see why the "new way" of selling a subscription model makes a lot of sense. Selling subscriptions completely revolutionizes and changes your business. Every day when you wake up, you should say to yourself "I'm going to sell some subscriptions today" – even before you have your first cup of coffee!

CASE STUDY – Jordan Powers Sells High Ticket and Subscriptions

Let's look at a real life example – one that we discussed before. CloudPano member Jordan Powers sold to a community college in Minnesota. Here is his pricing scheme and how he went about this project:

<u>Set-Up Fee</u>: $8500 (which included going to location and photographing the college in 360°)

Virtual Tour Profit

<u>Subscription Fee</u>: $250 per month (which covers hosting, maintenance, and updates, including photographing new scenes when needed).

That means his year 1 value is $11,500, year 2 adds $3000 in subscription revenue, and if they stay on, year 3 is an additional $3000. This means the 3-year value of this one customer is $17,500. And that's just for one customer.

Now let's hypothetically play out a scenario where Jordan acquires 30 customers at these price points. His 3-year value is $525,000. And that's just for 30 customers.

We have members in our VTPS (Virtual Tour Profit System, our high-level accelerator program) who are selling subscriptions as their business model, and they're basing their pricing schemes on the specific niche they choose.

It's important to put together your offer alongside the client. This is how you structure an offer that makes sense to the client and is lucrative for you as a provider.

We mentioned Heather Eakins, who is a good example of this. She was charging $400 plus $25 per month per floor plan unit to multi-family apartment complexes. And she would charge an extra $1000 for an amenity space. Since each location averages 3 floor plan units plus an amenity space, and she sold up to 30 complexes, she was earning $100,000 a year from this pricing structure. And what's more impressive was how she was able to close another similar contract (she did it twice in 90 days).

It's all about targeting the right market, structuring offers together, and then going about the sales process in a professional way that makes sense to them and to you.

If you want to learn more about offer structures and get surrounded by a community in this field, you need to join VTPS today. Visit virtualtourprofit.com and watch the free training.

TANNER'S RECURRING REVENUE CASE STUDY

We also have a VTPS member named Tanner, and he has a different and interesting model which he shared on our Thursday weekly support call. He charges a subscription to event venues, and offers three tiered pricing options:

Tier #1: $50 per month – Just the virtual tour on CloudPano

Tier #2: $100 per month – Includes Google Analytics Integration (which is available through CloudPano)

Tier #3: $150 a month – Includes extra features and Google Street View Upload.

Virtual Tour Profit

Most of Tanner's clients go for the middle tier, and he's signed up 20 clients already. Plus, he waives the set-up fee if the customer can refer him to 3 business owners.

Tanner is located in Ohio, in an area where very few people are shooting VR tours, so he has a massive advantage with this technology. His sales tactic is really smart. Tanner calls up prospective clients and tells them that he's coming to their area to shoot 360° virtual tours of events and places. He explains that he wants to shoot their location to build his portfolio and all they need to do is to have someone turn the lights on and give him access. In most cases, clients are perfectly happy with this – after all, at this point he's not in selling mode.

What Tanner is doing is engineering a way to have the opportunity to meet with the client face-to-face. Tanner knows that his best skill is to sell to someone in person, so when he gets to the location and talks to the client, he can start a conversation about subscriptions.

He leverages analytics up front, because he knows they're likely paying for something similar already and without the need to pay for the actual photography, it's just a low monthly fee of $100 - $125 a month. That's very little in the events world, but in Tanner's world, it creates a portfolio of valuable clients that pay him every month. His goal is to get 100 clients paying a monthly subscription. He understands that mathematically, if he can do that, he'll make somewhere around $125,000 a year in passive income. So, by not getting greedy with set up fees, he plays the long game, and it's paying off handsomely.

This is an example of an entrepreneur taking on a trending technology, assigning a great business model, and building equitable value that makes his business very valuable to a buyer one day.

Or he can just pocket the cash flow and enjoy the revenue every month he gets from his clients. But Tanner's business model doesn't end there. In the long term, he will come back to each of his clients and sell them marketing services and high-ticket add-ons. Instead of starting his pitch with high-ticket offers, he's first gaining their trust, building a relationship, and showing them that he can provide a product of value that they love. In time, the clients will see that the product is resulting in more leads and more sales, and it's at that point that upselling is an easy and natural next step.

Copy and paste this strategy and get started today!

CHAPTER 7

Creating Freedom

The Power of Outsourcing

Outsourcing is fundamental to every entrepreneur. In fact, some may even go as far as to define an "entrepreneur" as a "professional outsourcer". Quite simply, outsourcing is resourcing and finding activities in your business that you can have someone else do for a fee and you keep the margin. Outsourcing should be done at whatever level or scale your business is currently running, and it's been truly revolutionary for my own entrepreneurial journey. After some resistance, as I got better at outsourcing, I began to realize that I, myself, had been the biggest constraint on my business growth.

While you're growing your business, it's important to learn and understand the many different skills required as a business owner, whether they are understanding sales, marketing, fulfilment, or building the customer journey. While these are important skill sets, many of the actual day-to-day work of these elements can be done by someone else at a fee, and this frees you up to focus on scaling your business - your core focus. Whether you're doing a local VR digital marketing service or you're trying to grow a global brand like CloudPano.com. If I had to pick one skill set that's most important for an entrepreneur to have success, it's learning how to outsource effectively and efficiently.

I mentioned earlier that I personally had some resistance as a young entrepreneur when implementing outsourcing, and this "push back" is common amongst many in the early stages of building a business. There are many initial thoughts of resistance that come to our mind…"but I can do this myself and pocket the money", "no one will produce the same quality as me" etc.
Recognize these thoughts? Let's take a look at some of the ideas and see if we can overcome them together.

QUALITY CONTROL

As you're putting out a product with your brand behind it, you'll no doubt be concerned about quality control. Maybe you'll be thinking "no one can ever create the same quality as I can", which in part is the same as "no one else has the level of skill I do" and "no one else will take as much care as I do." These are reasonable concerns, but there are simple answers to these questions and they require an amount of humility (which, I know, is not always easy for the business owner!)

Firstly, there ARE people out there who can do just as good a job, possibly even better than you. The world is filled with many talented and skilled people. There are many people with incredible skills in specific areas, but they may not be entrepreneurs like you. So while you are very good at multiple skill sets as a business person, there are certain people who *specialize*.

Finding these brilliant freelancers and building a formidable team can add great value to your business. However, yes, you may be right that you may struggle to find someone that matches your quality. But, the business argument for this is that it is better to have an 80% quality solution than having to spend 10 or 20 hours of your own time making up that extra 20%.

Virtual Tour Profit

The great masters of art understood this. Did you know that artists like Da Vinci and Michelangelo did not produce their great artworks alone? They designed and planned their paintings and murals, and added the finishing touches, but the bulk of the work – the preparations of the surfaces, the formulations of the materials, the exacting measurements and the hundreds of thousands of tiny brushstrokes – these were done by their "students".

Was a young art student going to paint as well as the grandmaster? Of course not! But these artists understood that if they did everything themselves, they would not be able to complete their ambitious projects. So, in addition to being great artists, they were also great *educators*. As I say in our business, "the quality of your output will be directly related to the quality of my instructions."

You can see examples of this in all spheres of big business. For example, Bill Gates, Ex CEO of Microsoft, was renowned for being a great programmer. He was no doubt a better programmer than any of the thousands of developers that he hired. But imagine if he had decided to do all the work himself? In his lifetime he wouldn't have likely gotten much further than his humble start up. If you read the biographies of the world's great entrepreneurs, one of the common threads amongst all of them is that they see themselves as educators. They focus their energy on *empowering* other people.

To set up your outsourcing plan, as the "master controller" of your business, you need to cast a vision for your entire operation – how are you going to run your team up front? How are you going to photograph on location? How are you going to post-process your photos? How are you going to create virtual tours on CloudPano? How are you going to deliver them to clients, send invoices, set up subscriptions, manage your customers?

The worst case scenario is you create a great business that gives lots of leads and customers and sales, but it takes all of your time. That is a bad scenario because the freedom that you seek and are longing is now farther away because of your success without a proper outsourcing plan.

360° PHOTOGRAPHY

For your 360° photography on location, you can hire a young photographer who works by the hour. We do this. We pay $10 an hour to a young college student who is looking for some work, a side business, a side job to pay for just some general expenses in their life. We send out the contract employee to the location, show them how to use a 360° camera, give them expectations of what we want and desire, what to avoid and how to have success on location, how to deliver the photos to us, and how to do it all by themselves. And we pay them by the hour.

There are many kinds of people that can be easily trained. Look for someone who is young and often has a camera in their hands.

POST-PROCESSING

Once the 360° photos are taken, they need to go through post-processing in order to make adjustments and tweaks to bring out the very best quality and have that slick professional finish. Post-processing can take up a lot of your time and it can easily, effectively, and economically be outsourced. Countries with lower economies (where the US dollar is heavy) such as Vietnam, Philippines, India etc. are excellent places to look for post-processing freelancers. There are endless freelancers or "shops" in these countries with very high-end skills and great talent for editing and creating impressive quality photos from your on-location files. Given the comparative weakness of their currency and lower costs-of-living, you can negotiate an excellent rate – sometimes $1-$3 per photo or even less if you are sending bulk work. A big plus is that because these countries are in different time zones, your editor will be working on your photos while you sleep. You wake up to the project finished!

Today, it's easier than ever to connect to these talents online, whether through a Google search or via one of the many popular freelancing websites (freelancer.com, Upwork.com, Fiverr etc.). Of course the quality of works varies greatly, so you will need to test out a few editors until you find one that produces the right quality at the right price and is good at communicating. Inside VTPS, we give a resource to our members of approved post processing providers, expert photo editors, and photo editing teams that we like and trust.

VIRTUAL ASSISTANTS

You need to get really good at outsourcing your administrative activities. Admin can quickly become overwhelming, and outsourcing admin to the right person is truly invaluable. Admin activities include everything that needs to be done in a business day-to-day that's not about selling or creating your product. The long list includes answering the phone, sending out invoices, sending out calendar invites, updating spreadsheets, managing schedules, handling your customer service email, bookkeeping, building lists of possible clients etc.

The concept of a VA (virtual assistant) has become extremely popular in recent years. A virtual assistant means that you can hire an assistant anywhere in the world and they can do all these tasks online. For example, for your phone line. You can sign up for Google Voice and calls can be forwarded to your VA. I can highly recommend hiring a VA in the Philippines. There are many people in the Philippines looking for this kind of work. In general, the culture of friendliness, hard work, and loyalty make for excellent virtual assistants.

In addition, given the country's struggling economy, a VA from the Philippines is very affordable. Costs can be anywhere from $4-$5 an hour. You can hand off all of your administrative activities – it will be worth every cent!

Virtual Tour Profit

A typical workflow could look like this:

-VA takes an order

-VA instructs 360° photographer

-360° photographer sends files to VA

-VA sends files to post-processing team

-VA pays 360° photographer and post-processing editor through PayPal

-VA delivers link to your client's white labeled on CloudPano

As you can see, this makes life a lot easier for you, and with all the time saved, you can focus on scaling your business. So put simply, you do the sales, your team does the fulfillment. It's a winning formula!

WEB DESIGN

It's a great idea to outsource your web design. Just as with the previous task, this can be economically outsourced to talent in foreign countries. Ukraine and other Eastern European countries are well known for their web designing skills, as is Vietnam. There are many popular and inexpensive platforms for creating a website, such as WordPress or Weebly or Webflow. I'd recommend not obsessing over your website, and rather put your energy into getting customers. Outsourcing your web design will allow you to get rolling quickly.

MARKETING

All of your marketing activities can be outsourced, and there are very skilled and experienced people out in the marketplace. For example, you can outsource funnel building. You could get a freelancer to build a landing page, create some animations, capture leads etc. Advertising can be outsourced as well, once you have a bigger budget – for example, you can hire an agency to set up and maintain a local Facebook campaign.

Any type of digital media service is becoming a commodity in the global market. There are endless freelancers online offering graphic design. Want a logo? A sales sheet? A promo PDF? These can all be done quickly and cheaply by finding a graphic designer online through freelancing platforms like Fiverr or Upwork. You can have these things up and running professionally, beautifully, and delivered in front of your clients without having to even think. They'll send you mock ups. You pick your favorite one, you can get multiple colors, versions and formats created. In my case, I needed a logo for CloudPano.com. I found a freelancer online, gave her instructions, showed her examples of other logos I liked, and $20 and a matter of days later she presented me with our logo, the one we still use today. And in addition, she sent me versions in ten different colors.

COLD CALLING

Cold calling can be outsourced too! There is an entire industry dedicated to what's called "Appointment Setting". It's been proven that people respond better to calls than emails, and if you have a list of thousands of business owners, it's simply not possible for you to individually call each one of them. If you can find a shop that knowshow to do a good job with your script, you can have a team of people making cold calls for you and filling up your calendar with appointments. In the early stages of your business, it's vital that you do the selling yourself so that you can gain knowledge about the industry and discover what works and what doesn't. But once you have reached a certain size – and once your prospective client list has reached a certain size - it can be effective to outsource your cold calling to a team or to a sales rep.

BUILDING YOUR MACHINE

Handing off the sales piece of your business is oneof the hardest things – after all, your sales is the life-blood of your business. In the beginning you'll need to "pound the pavement" and take full responsibility for sales. You'll need to dig into the validation of your business, understand the intricacies of your market and determine your price points. Once you have all these elements figured out, you can move onto creating a "customer acquisition machine" – thinking about how you're going to get customers into your calendar every single day and what pieces of that funnel framework you'll need to consistently book folks on your calendar.

You need software that can connect with your calendar so that a lead can download your free resources, download your case studies, and then if they want to work with you (which they will, after you do a good job showing off your marketing service and example demos) they're going to book a time automatically on your calendar to go over a demo. This demo is called a "strategy call", and you want to have this entire funnel built out so the calendar fills automatically. When your calendar is full, you can then outsource your sales.

As a VR entrepreneur, you want to create a "machine" – a machine that folks can plug in and use in any environment, any niche, any location. A well-designed machine will allow you to expand into new markets, niches, and locations. You will, at some point, be able to hand off, and maybe even hand off completely, the sales to your VA or to your team.

Virtual Tour Profit

So, what might that look like? Your customer comes from your online advertisement, books a time, buys a project. Your team creates the project and fulfills the deliverable, at which time your VA sends out an invoice and follows up with payment.

Congratulations! You have a freedom business and a very profitable enterprise that can scale. This is your goal, and this is the power of outsourcing.

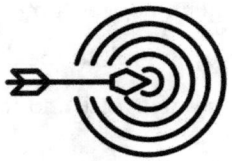

CHAPTER 8

The Importance Of One Niche

Building a track record

For many starting out in building a 360° Virtual Tour business, one of the first questions is about niches – which to focus on and how many to approach? At first, it's only natural to think about what contacts you have, what networks you're connected to, which niches you have access to through family, friends, and colleagues. Typically, you'll end up with quite a big list of niches and industries, maybe 5 or even 10. And they may get you excited – so much opportunity, how could you go wrong! But...there's a Golden Rule of entrepreneurship whatever business you may be in:

Target one niche at a time

That may sound counter-intuitive. Surely you should take advantage of all the opportunities you can get? But this rule has great wisdom, and we'll look through the reasons why it makes sense.

1. FOCUS

   One of my business mantras is *"Focus is your friend and distraction is your enemy."* Whichever niche you choose, there will always be moments where you are challenged. Each niche has its own set of problems and obstacles, and it requires dedication and focus to work through these and find solutions. Having too many opportunities can become a dangerous distraction. It's human nature – when we have many options, as soon as one presents a difficulty we want to move to another option in the hope it will be easier. This is a dangerous trap and can leave you overwhelmed and confused.

2. BOUNDARIES FOR CREATIVITY

As you go after your niche, you want to be able to focus on one problem for one customer, one at a time. When you do this, you can build out the same marketing materials, using the same logos, using the same examples that you have in the past. This makes marketing to that niche much faster and easier. You'll have to create new offers every time you get a new niche or you go after a new type of client.

3. TRACK RECORD

You can leverage your track record with a relevant niche to your client. What this means is if you help RV dealer A sell more RVs a month, well, RV dealer B will hear or read or watch that case study and go, wow, I really like that they're already working with RV dealers and helping them! This feels relevant to me. And I feel like this service or technology will be helpful in *my* journey to grow *my* RV dealership. So by having a track record within a niche, you'll be able to include in your marketing "before and after" case studies that are relevant to your potential client.

4. MEASURABLE RESULTS

Having a track record in a specific niche will mean that you can have measurable results. This is because you know, within the industry, the approximate value of one customer. Because you've been working inside that boundary of creativity within that one niche, you now know the approximate value that you can project from a client using you.

5. TARGETED MARKETING

Focusing on a specific niche allows you to use targeted words and phrases in your advertising and marketing copy. This is vital in getting customers' attention. Let's imagine you're in the food court at the center of a mall. You stand on the table and you yell out "Hey, I have an offer! I have a Virtual Tour Business!" and you list all of the great services you can offer, "360 photos! Fully interactive ad videos! Cloud Pano Live!" The result? You'll get zero customers, zero attention (except perhaps from mall security!). But why is that? After all, you're surrounded by a mall filled with different people of all kinds. It's because it's not *targeted*, it's too general, and the general doesn't get attention.

Imagine that a stranger comes up to you and says "Hey, can I tell you something?" You'll likely wave them away. But what if your name is Lucy, and that same stranger says "Hey, Lucy, can I tell you something?" Now they've got your attention. Why? Because it's not general, they've used your name, they are specifically wanting to talk to *you*.

It's the same thing within a niche. If you call out to a specific business owner type, you're going to get their attention. So if I call out to a fitness studio owner, there's a very specific person with specific pains, interests, and particular problems that you'll help them solve through your marketing services. They'll pay attention if you call out to them. Think back to when you were a teenager. Teenagers tend to divide themselves into specific groups – skaters, jocks, cheerleaders, star trek fans etc. the list is endless! Now imagine you wanted to join a specific group? How do you do this? Step number one is language and jargon. Using specific words, phrases, and jokes signal to a group that you are one of them. In business it's just the same – we're still teenagers, just grown up! If you focus on one niche, you will get to learn the industry jargon, and this will allow you to be seen as part of the group. As an example, in the car sales niche there's a long list of secret words and phrases. A customer that signs on the first offer is called an "Ace", a car buyer that walks into the dealership with the latest car advertisement in his hand is called a "Paperboy". An "Atomic Pencil" is when the manager writes an extremely high first offer, and you never want to see the words "ATPOS" – car salesmen sometimes write this on a customer's trade-in appraisal sheet and it stands for "A Total Piece of"…(I can't remember what the S was for). So, understanding the secret jargon and terminology of your niche can really help target your marketing and advertising, and guarantee you attention. Learning the lingo can take time and experience, so this is why focusing on a single niche is to your advantage.

6. EXPERTISE

When you target one niche, you quickly become an expert. You are razor sharp and focused on that specific industry. You know what they need, their value, their customers. And you know what to say and what not to say. It works like this:

The more general you are, the less attention, the less resonance you're going to get. The more specific you are, the more response you're going to get.

This is true in sales, it's true in marketing, it's true in socializing, it's just true across the board. And the more specific you are, the more success you're going to have.

7. REPEATABLE OFFERS

You want to create repeatable offers that are easy to distribute if someone asks for a price. You should be able to send out a slide deck with pricing because it fits their needs, and you can even quickly change it because it has all the marketing copy for that specific niche. You can do this copy and paste because they're all the same niche and you pretty much know what the offer is going to end up being.

WHAT NICHE TO CHOOSE?

When you're starting out, you'll need to make that critical decision of which niche you will focus on. It's worth putting solid time and thought into your choice, as it's an important decision, but at the end of the day, it's vital to actually make that choice. Make a jump. Too much back and forth can cause paralysis in making a decision, so although it requires research, don't avoid taking the leap when you see an opportunity. Here are some of the things to take into consideration when doing your research:

CURRENT NETWORK

Who have you already built social equity with? What niches are your friends, family, and colleagues in? Maybe you even have a connection that could be an affiliate partner that already has connections in a certain industry? Tapping into the knowledge of someone you know is far more useful and expedient than cold-researching an industry as an outsider. Speak to your connections, have a conversation about their industry, what their problem points are, what their values are, whether they think your services would be helpful, what they would pay for a 360° Virtual Tour? Tapping into the knowledge of your existing network will help you get started exponentially faster.

THE RIGHT FIT

It's important to ask yourself, what do I enjoy doing? Who do I enjoy speaking to? This is extremely important because once you focus on a niche this will very quickly become your day-to-day world. For example, I'm not big into fashion. So if I was to go into the fashion space, I probably wouldn't be excited to speak to those types of prospects every day. But, being from Texas, and perhaps being a little bit of a redneck, I can talk to an RV dealer all day. They speak my kind of language and the product is interesting for me to discuss day-in–and-out. So you have to do a personal inventory of who you enjoy speaking to. What industries do you enjoy being a part of? This is an important thing to consider whenever you are targeting your niche.

A GENUINE NEED

Another question that you need to ask is whether there is a realistic need and value in this specific industry for 360° Virtual Tours? Your service needs to provide a real value to a real problem, so this can't be a matter of wishful thinking. Not every niche is suitable for Virtual Tours, so if you cannot solve a real problem, you're not going to have any transactions.

SALES CYCLE LENGTH

It's important to look at the sales cycle length of an industry. For example, certain industries, especially public entities that are tax dollar funded, have long sales cycles. These kinds of sales can be lucrative, so I'm not suggesting you totally avoid them, but you need to be aware that these niches will be frustrating for you as a start up. It will be challenging to get meetings and challenging to get commitments as you'll be at the mercy of their budgeting schedules. If you aretargeting a niche with a long sales cycle, this can be a reason for targeting two niches – one with a long sales cycle, and one that you can get commitments from more easily and regularly to aid your cash flow.

CUSTOMER ACCESS

Do you have access to the customer? This is really important because the bigger the company size, the more difficult it will be to get in front of the boss, the decision-maker. Large corporations generally place many obstacles in the way of a sales person before they can get a meeting with the actual decision-maker. So realize that this is going to be a challenging sales process. That doesn't mean it can't be done. Decision-makers within a large organization are used to sales calls coming their way, they're used to booking times and evaluating deals. And of course, large organizations often mean large and lucrative orders. But it's important to be aware if this is going to be a challenge and of how much extra time and effort it will take to get a meeting and a decision.

If that kind of challenge doesn't sound like the right thing for you, if you don't want to spend days and weeks chasing up to get a meeting, then small business owners are a great place to start. If you call up a small business, typically the owner will be there. And the owner is the one with the power to make a decision on the spot without anyone else's approval. It's every small business owner's job to spend money on their business to help it grow, and it's your job to help them grow…so bingo! You're in an easy position to connect to the right person without much fuss.

TRANSACTION SIZE

Another question that you need to ask is "what is their transaction size?" "Transaction size" is not how much money you can get from them. It's what the value of a new customer is to the client. For example, in the college niche, a student will pay $40,000 to sign up. So the size of each transaction is $40,000. The higher the transaction size, the higher you can charge the client for your help in acquiring a transaction. For example, you may work with a manufacturer that sells each product for a million dollars. In that case, it's easy to justify a $10,000 contract to create a virtual tour of their manufacturing facility.

There's a curious thing that happens in business that I can't quite explain why, but it's how it works. Generally, the higher the transaction size, the less competition you will have. This is likely because people see lower-ticket items as easier to sell. The human brain naturally thinks "If I go after the smallest ticket niche or industry, I'll be able to get more transactions and sales will be easier." Oftentimes, the lower-priced niches are just as hard to sell, if not harder than the higher priced ones! So keep that in mind as you're writing down and picking your niches to target.

SUBSCRIPTIONS AND UP-SELLING

When you are doing your research, take into consideration whether this niche is appropriate for charging a subscription. As discussed previously, the subscription model completely changes the value of your business. Previously, we covered the power of adding marketing services, selling lead generation, and up-selling a variety of add-on services. So ask yourself whether this is a niche that will value these additional services. If they do, it will be much easier to increase the customer value because customers that buy from you are the best to rebuy. So can you up-sell them, or will they just be a one-off type customer?

PRODUCT OWNERSHIP

Another great question to ask is do they own the product or are they just borrowing it? This can make a big difference to your interactions, and what I mean by it is this: Let's consider a small business owner. He owns his products. He's paid for them, taken an investment risk, and therefore he is passionate and dedicated to do all that he can to make them sell. Conversely, an estate agent is in a different position. They are "borrowing" the product. They're selling a property for someone, but they don't own the property, and therefore they are less likely to invest in the product and are less emotionally attached as well. Between these two, you've got a much higher chance of getting a "yes" from the small business owner.

CONCLUSION

There are plenty of amazing niches out there, and many that will be perfectly suited to you. We give our Cloud Pano members a list of over 2500 niches to get your juices flowing! So there's no need to be thinking out of thin air, no need to Google "small business ideas". In this chapter we've looked at how to evaluate your niche and what questions to ask when you're making your decision. But these aren't hard and fast rules. If you have three niches you are targeting, that's OK too. But when it comes to an automatic email campaign, you're going to be saying relatively the same things with a few names or companies or emails swapped out. So it's much easier to scale your prospecting when you pick a niche. Your main goal is to have a successful case study within a niche, a success story that you can use in your pitch to future prospects. So do all the research you want. Have fun researching. Learn some cool stuff, have conversations with different people in different industries. But overall, <u>make a choice</u> and go get some ROI, a success story. Whatever it takes to get moving ahead. That's what you do first. So make a choice and let's get started!

CHAPTER 9

Using Google Maps To Convert The Best Customers

In the previous chapter we talked about picking a niche. In this chapter I am going to help you narrow your choices.

Google My Business is of great value to you as an entrepreneur, and in turn is also of great value to <u>every</u> small business owner. So, let's take a look at the tool and see how it can help you.

Any time a small business owner starts a new business (and that includes you too!), one of the first channels they want to get activated locally is Google Maps. This is done through visiting google.com/business, where you can set up what's called a Google My Business listing page. This allows you to set up your listing with all of your information, such as your name, phone number, website, images, services and products etc.

One of the features on Google My Business, is the ability to add a Google Street View interior walk-through, and having this in your listing greatly increases customer engagement. This is vital because the only way for a small business owner to add a Google Street View interior walk-through on their Google Maps listing is with 360° photos. You need access to a 360° photographer. This means that every small business owner who's starting their business, and getting going with their marketing, has a specific period of time when they're looking for a 360° Google Street View photographer! This is where you come in with your 360° virtual tour ability, and create quick value for a small business owner, build a relationship, and then work on other marketing services and avenues to help them achieve their goals.

In the past, when you first created a Google My Business page, you would get a physical postcard at the address to confirm you owned the Google My Business listing. This postcard would arrive in your mailbox within a few days and would also have a confirmation code – a way for Google to confirm that you exist. Once you type in your activation code, you would gain access to all the Google My Business features and you could add all of your business details. The process changed post-COVID, but the principals are the same.

There are many options for adding your company's information. From reviews to details about your products and services and contact information, to 360° photos and video, as well as your latest updates. Adding this information is vital, and the more details provided, the better chance at gaining new organic leads. But adding all this information, working out what keywords to use, and competing with other local businesses on Google Maps takes time, and can be a headache for a small business owner. This is great news for you! It's an opportunity for you to leverage your knowledge and expertise of Google Maps, Google My Business, and Google Street View to build value, rapport, and sell services to your clients.

THE PERFECT OPENING

Google Maps is a great way to start a conversation with a prospective client. It's a common ground between you and a business owner because everyone knows Google Maps. Everyone has used it themselves, and a business owner will know that it's a good idea to be featured there. So, it's an easy sell and doesn't require a lot of explaining. Once you sign up a client on 360° photography for Google Maps, you'll be in a good position to further that relationship by offering additional services, with Google My Business optimization as the next logical step.

GOOGLE MY BUSINESS OPTIMIZATION

What is Google My Business optimization? Essentially, it's a simple service where you jump into someone's Google My Business page and optimize their listing for the keywords they are targeting. Keywords are an extremely important part of the Google game, and having the right keywords is vital to appearing in searches and attracting customers.

To explain the importance of keywords, I like to use the analogy of a taco shop (perhaps because as I'm writing this, I'm getting hungry!). A taco shop will have a range of products – they have burritos, they have fajitas, they have bean soup. They'll probably want to rank for "breakfast tacos", "lunch", and "Mexican food", as these are the typical terms that hungry local folks will be searching for. If you have these keywords on your listing within a certain radius, you will appear higher in the search results than other nearby taco shops that don't. Google is very smart and sophisticated with how they match searches to businesses, and as a marketer, you need to cast a wide net for your clients. You'll want to appear in every search term that you can. This means that beyond the common terms, you'll also need to get creative. For example, in addition to "chicken fajita", you may also want to add something like "best chicken fajita in the downtown area" or "best value for money chicken fajita". This means that your client's listing requires keyword-rich services inside all the tools in Google My Business, and it presents a great opportunity for you.

Within Google My Business, there is a tab that says "services". Clicking on that tab allows you to add in all the different services and locations you offer those services. What's great about this is if I offer burritos in a certain town in Texas, I can place those keywords in the services or products tab, and then add a helpful amount of information in a paragraph about that specific burrito. So, if someone's looking for gluten free tacos, and that's something your client offers, you want to have that keyword inside their listing.

HOW TO SELL THE SERVICE

The way you sell this service is simple. Your opening question should be "Do you want to rank locally when folks search for your type of business?" Of course, everytime, their answer will be yes, of course! You can then demonstrate to them by typing in some relevant keywords into Google, and showing them how their competitors rank higher, or how they don't even appear in the search results at all. This **will get** any business owner's attention.

You can't always guarantee that you're going to be able to appear locally on Google Maps based on how you optimize the listing, but when you're talking about SEO (Search Engine Optimization), you can do a lot with very little and make a big difference because typically the competition isn't thinking at this deep of a level.

Search Engine Optimization at a local level is much easier to compete than at a national level. Getting "best burrito in America" is going to be next to impossible because you're competing with literally thousands of businesses, and SEO at this level is a complex and high-budget game. But to compete locally is a whole lot simpler, and getting good results is a lot more realistic, as there is only a small pool of competition locally.

An interesting statistic to consider (and an interesting point to explain to a client) is that around 40% of Google Maps searches are people looking for items nearby. That means it's a huge deal to be ranking highly at a local level.

WHY SEO IS IMPORTANT TO YOU

All this talk of SEO and keywords may have you thinking "I don't want to be an SEO person", "I don't care about that, I want to be a great photographer or a great marketer". However, to be successful as a photographer, marketer, and salesperson, understanding SEO at a basic level is a very worthwhile skill and service to offer. It's the language that business owners are speaking, and it's a perfect way to "get your foot in the door". SEO and Google ranking is important to every business owner, so it should be important to you!

HOW IT'S DONE

CloudPano is your secret weapon for doing this all super easily and quickly. What you'll do is go on location and take a few photos, perhaps four or five. You then go back to your computer and search for that business within your CloudPano Pro Plus account in the Street View. Once you've found that business, you can upload your 360° photos and create a walkthrough experience in Google Maps. CloudPano makes this an easy process to fulfil through its Google Maps integration.

To get yourself familiar with the process, you can start with creating a listing for your own 360° Virtual Tour business. Once you've done that and spent the time working the steps out, you'll be in a position to offer the service and your knowledge to business owners.

When beginning a discussion with a prospective client, and building rapport, you have an opportunity to create what's called "expert positioning". You can do this by offering to help them for free. It's part of a longer game strategy, and there's nothing wrong with telling your client what to do and how to do it.

You may be thinking "but then my client won't need me!" But here's what's likely to happen. You'll start taking them through the process, you'll explain all the Google tools and features – how you can add a town name into their services tab, how they can embed keywords into their images, how they can tag actual coordinates into the metadata of each photo…

As you continue to explain all the options, your client is likely to be both impressed and excited, and will start to feel overwhelmed. They'll think "I need all these things as soon as possible, but this looks like a lot of work, and I don't know if I'll remember all these things!" It's at this point that you can offer your services, and there's a good chance they'll convert right there and then.

The actual Google My Business optimization can be completed by your virtual assistant or a writer for a few bucks. This way, you can have an entire secondary service that you have added into the core business model of your business.

THE SOLUTION FIRST TO PROBLEM FRAMEWORK

When you think about the selling process, you need to use this analogy. It's called the Solution First To Problem Framework. This is very important in your selling process, your marketing, and how you go about your campaigns.

Most marketers think that if you talk about the problem, if you really build up the problem and then offer the solution as a service, you'll be able to make transactions. In some cases this is true, but I want you to think differently.

When you're speaking to a customer, **give them the solution**. When you give them the solution, a **new** problem arises.

Let's look at an analogy that will make this easy to understand. When you're hungry, you go to the kitchen. What do you do? You get some food, you eat the food, and you feel good afterwards. You just took care of your hunger problem, but with that solution, a new problem arises. What's the new problem? You now have a dirty dish which needs to be cleaned. For that you need soap and a sponge, which means you need to go to the store to purchase soap and a sponge so you can clean. By finding a solution to your first problem (hunger), you've created a second problem that needs a solution (cleaning up).

It works the same way in business. If a business owner doesn't have a Google My Business account and listing, they're not going to need your services of optimization. If you give them free advice and help them set up a Google My Business, you're giving them a solution that will then lead to a problem. Before they didn't need optimization, but now that they have a Google My Business account. Suddenly there is a new need! This is how you apply the Solution First To Problem.

And that new problem is exactly what you can offer help with. This is when you can profit.

Be thinking about how you can offer free help and give away solutions to create a new problem that you can solve.

CHAPTER 10

Advertising That Converts

Advertising is an important scaling tool as a service provider. It's the accelerator to your validated business model. It helps you quickly put gasoline on your **fire**.

Before you start advertising, you need a validated offer. Focus on prospecting activities: making calls, sending emails, and having client meetings. This is a vital first step in the beginning and needs to be done, but prospecting requires energy and calories. It's inexpensive – but getting started takes up your time.

Advertising is the opposite. It doesn't take calories, doesn't take much energy, but can be expensive. Advertising requires patience and lots of testing, and it takes time to build up experience to understand and discover what works today.

COPYWRITING

To get your advertising to convert is all about the copy – the words you choose and the messaging. Think of it as salesmanship in print. Advertising grabs attention and sends someone down a path to a conversion. Copywriting has the power to completely change your business.

Here are some interesting statistics to show the importance of copywriting:

80% of people only read the headline

This means your headline, which is only a few short words, needs to be carefully engineered to grab your prospect by the throat (metaphorically).

If your headline doesn't attract immediate attention and curiosity, then it doesn't matter if you have the best message and the best offer that exists.

Your headline needs to call out to your niche so the right person will engage with your advertisement. Be clear in how you can help them. For example, if your niche is a property manager, you might want to say something like "Are you a property manager? Do you want to fill up all your leases to 100% occupancy?" or "Do you need more showing and applications?" This kind of headline is more enticing than mentioning your service – like 360° virtual tours.

You can deliver your solution later in the body copy.

Most readers only consume 20% of content on a page

If your reader decides to continue reading after the headline, you should be aware the majority will not read your full copy. So your job is to be so good that they have to keep reading.

Messages that are written at a third-grade reading level receive 36% more responses

Using simple words and phrases is more effective with advertising. Avoid complex words and keep your message straightforward and easy to understand.

CASE STUDIES X COPYWRITING = EXPLOSIVE GROWTH

Earlier We discussed the importance of having case studies (track records) of measurable results. This is exponentially more important in the advertising phase of your business. Your customers want results, and they want to see proof. Show proof in your ads. Show how you already solved this same problem in the past. And show your long list of clients who are wildly happy from working with you.

If you have a consistent track record, you're going to be able to sell faster, get more attention, and close more clients.

This means every time your clients have success, make sure you **document** what happened. What was their problem? What steps did you take to get them to success? What were their results?

These stories and documentation of the "before and after state" can be used to show prospective clients that you get results and have a **track record** to back it up.

Having client testimonials is also very useful. Once you've done a good job for a client, he/she is at the point where they are excited about their results. Ask the client if they would be willing to give you a short testimonial quote. This simple sentence or two is gold in your advertising.

I am known for asking my customers to stop what they are doing and shoot a selfie video sharing their success. This is raw, real, and more believable than a polished testimonial. It works.

A.I.D.A.

When creating your advertising copy, you should follow the copy writing framework called A.I.D.A. This stands for Attention, Interest, Desire, Action.

<u>Attention</u>

Your first task is to grab the reader's attention as quickly as possible. To do this, you need to call out to them – speak to their niche. You need to point to them, so they **know** your offer is for *them*. If you've got a case study, you can use this for your headline.

Let's say your niche is car dealerships and you have a case study where you increased sales by $500,000 a month. Your headline could be something like "Increase your car dealership sales by $500,000 a month!" But you need to make sure that you can back this up with a **real** case study. Don't fake these numbers, or you will be crushed in your sales conversations deeper in the funnel.

During the attention phase of your ad, you need to be over-the-top and calling out to your audience. Here is a litmus test… "How do I get somebody to completely stop in their tracks, slam on their brakes, and read my ad?" If you are not passing this test – try again until you have a **banger**.

Interest

Now, once you have your prospect's attention, you need to build interest. This is done by engaging them with something that's interesting. For example, this could include case studies, stories, and testimonials showing the measurable results that you're already getting from your service in the specific location and with a specific utility. You're sharing the journey from your previous customers and how they achieved a transformation from working with you. This engages the niche, engages the prospect, and draws them into the ad once you have their interest.

Desire

Now it's time to build desire around that outcome they seek. You want to show their future life achieving their dream success. If they had everything they wanted, how would that look? Cast a vision for the same transformation your previous clients experienced. They can do it too; all they need is your framework and to follow the steps you explain. As the reader goes through this portion of the copywriting, they should get **excited!**

Remember, the ad should build value and be helpful! If you help them get a result, get them to change their thinking and shift their mind, you have created a desire that is ready to take action.

Action

The last phase of the A.I.D.A. formula is Action. The reader has now read your copy, they have shifted their thinking and are ready to move forward. Your next job is to show them the way. You now give an exact "call to action" that's simple and clear.

At this point you are giving step by step instructions. Do not assume your reader understands what to do next. The best CTAs are telling the reader **exactly what to do**.

So here are some examples...

Action: Email capture
CTA: "If you are ready to move forward, click this link here <link> add your email in the form and click the 'submit' button.

Action: Book a call
CTA: "To book a call, click this link <link> and fill out the form. When you submit your form, you will see our team calendar. Pick a time that works for you and click 'confirm.' I will see you on the call!"

See how I don't leave steps for chance? I **never** want to assume they will figure out the next steps. They won't. It does not matter how smart my audience; they need to be told what to do. And it's your job as a copywriter to make it clear.

INSPIRATION

A great source of inspiration I recommend is the famous copywriter, Gary Halbert. You can read his old ads and letters for free (Google 'The Gary Halbert Letters').

HEADLINE TIPS

Here are some tips to get your headlines to grab attention and convert.

Create tension. Compare and contrast two polarizing points and insert your reader in the middle. In order to illustrate this, here's an example I used on my wife.

My wife is a full-time mother. She loves taking care of my sons. She researches well. She's very engaged in every phase of their development. Nap time, feeding, any optimization for a child's development. She loves these topics, and she loves to talk about optimizing sleep for our kids etc. Since I know she is continually thinking about these topics, I threw a headline on her and tested the tension headline concept.

Virtual Tour Profit

Here is how it went…

I made up an article and I pretended to read it to her, "Why new mothers should bottle feed instead of breastfeed in month three of your baby's life." Her reaction was amazing. She stopped for a moment and asked me "What!? What are you talking about and where did you read this?"

Got her…

This headline called out to my target audience and created tension between two types of child-raising philosophies. One is breastfeeding and one is bottle feeding. New mothers are quickly faced with this decision in the early stages of their child's life. To some moms, it's an important decision. In the subculture of new mothers, this is quite a divided topic that has strong views and beliefs in both camps. **There is already tension there**.

So, I understand the market within that niche and understand the specific tension topics. I reverse engineer my headline by creating tension between those two camps, and this **will draw people** into my article. My wife agreed that the headline was effective and made her want to read more. She was a little disappointed that it was only a headline! Once you understand your niche, and once you have identified a clear problem that has two opposing "camps of thought", use it to create headlines with tension.

Please use this trick with responsibility. Be a marketer for good (not for evil).

PERFECTING YOUR AD

Good writing takes practice, time and focus. To create the perfect copy on your first attempt is difficult. Expect many iterations of your ads. Once you've written your drafts, share it with a friend and **read it out loud**. This will help you spot mistakes and correct stalls in your writing flow.

If you want to see campaigns I have written in the past, I recommend reviewing the Million Dollar Ads Templates inside the VTPS program. Learn more at the free webinar featured here: virtualtourprofit.com

CHAPTER 11

The Case Study Vault

Examples Success CloudPano Pro Plus Users

I'd like to share some success stories from members using CloudPano. You will be able to model their case studies and use them as inspiration.

Andy Crosier – Based in the UK, Andy sold a construction company who needed construction phasing done for their projects. They called it "the best insurance policy they could ever have" for their large projects. He was able to charge £ 2,500 pounds (about $3,500 USD) in the UK for this project.

Plus, it's an ongoing need, and therefore is an ongoing expense for this niche. Each time his client would complete a new phase of the project, they would need Andy to come to location and photograph the completed phases. In the construction niche, this type of project is less about quality of photos, and more about **proof** of performance. This means it's a low (sometimes zero) post-processing requirement.

Jordan Powers – We mentioned Jordan earlier in this book. He sold a community college for $8,500, plus a $250 a month subscription for 2 years. How he sold this project was very interesting. Before he sold this deal, he reached out to a local friend and marketer and partnered with him. His deal was very simple, 'You bring me some bigger clients – I give you a cut.' Well, a short time later they were pitching in front of a room of decision makers for the local community college in Mankato, Minnesota. As they were preparing for this meeting, Jordan took his Z1 camera and photographed some areas of the campus. This way he was able to take these into the meeting and have a **real world example** when explaining the service. Pricing this was also something I noted. He was **not** used to asking for large amounts of money for projects that took little time. So his partner Wes took over during this portion of the sale. Once they determined the value of a student was more than $16,000+ a year – the price became a much easier conversation. The idea here is simple. If the campus gets 1 more enrollment next year from the virtual tour - they just doubled their ROI on the project. It's an easy yes.

Plus, I recently received another message where Jordan closed another college deal for $18,000. It's safe to say he is getting comfortable charging high ticket. ☺

Mark Rutherford – Based in Michigan, Mark sold his mayor a $10,500 virtual tour, plus a $300 a year subscription. He was able to photograph his entire township for the mayor. His plan is to leverage this virtual tour to sell small business owners throughout that township. During his negotiation he was able to use his branding on the virtual tour. Once this deal was finalized, he was published in the paper 3 times. Soon after, his phone was exploding and his work pipeline was full.

I love this story because me and Mark connected on a CloudPano live video chat. I just gave him some small advice and didn't think much of it. During our call he had this "idea of selling his entire town." And for some reason he had this clarity about the project. A few days later he emailed me his success story. It was amazing to hear.

Peter Haney – A CloudPano Pro Plus user, he targets private schools, and is easily about to get a transaction value of $3,500 per private school. Photography time for a private school is 1 to 2 days max, and the creation of a virtual tour on CloudPano is a few hours. Private schools love these virtual tours and pay well to the right provider.

Rick Brazil – Rick is a professional architectural photographer who travels the country creating virtual tours for all types of industries. He recently sold a 30-location apartment contract using CloudPano. Rick was able to leverage his existing photography and video services and bolted on 360° into his product suite. Soon after I got a message from Rick where he commented "I just closed another 12-location nursing home project!" Rick is great at putting big deals together, and he delivers on CloudPano.com

Julie Shinabery from Charlotte – Julie was able to sell a 35 apartment complex contract by leveraging and using CloudPano as a Pro Plus user. Julie started in the Real Estate Photography niche and wanted to expand to bigger and better clients. She still serves both markets well, and even writes for the National Association of Realtors blog. And she is a member of VTPS.

Barry Smith – Barry is pastor-turned-VT-entrepreneur, who has sold a large health facility on a virtual tour, post pandemic. Barry is a member of VTPS. As he put together his offer alongside his client, he was careful to ask which service needed custom content based on the services they offered. As you determine specific services and features your clients want to highlight, you can easily add video and photography into your offer and watch the price increase to meet those needs. He was able to charge them a generous fee to create a robust health facility virtual tour.

Robert from Tre' Lynn Photography – Robert was able to sell an equestrian center a virtual tour on CloudPano for $10,000. He showed me the tour, which started from an aerial 360° photo taken from his drone. This tour highlights the entire facility, and he said the client "LOVED IT." Next he is targeting large universities in the area to continue collecting high ticket virtual tour clients.

Simon Woolley – Simon is out of Australia. He was able to sell his first client just from a few customer interactions. This first customer paid him around $1,500 to photograph their real estate development projects quickly.

Steven from Clover Sky Media - Steve sold five business owners in five days. With combining his video and virtual tour skills, he was able to quickly close these clients by utilizing our VTPS problem and pain selling framework.

Tanner – A VTPS member we've mentioned earlier in this book. Tanner has built an impressive portfolio of virtual tour subscription clients in his business in a short time. He already has 20 customers paying him subscriptions, and he upsells them Google Analytics and/or Google Street view alongside his 360° virtual tour offer. He targets event spaces and lets his clients refer him to the next buyer.

Heather Eakins – A VTPS member we also mentioned earlier in this book. She's sold over $200,000 in multi family property manager and development projects. It's around 60 locations. She told me she can photograph three locations in one day. Also, by the way, she had no previous photography experience. This again shows you do not need to be a photography expert to become a VR entrepreneur.

Ron Kroger – I mentioned Ron in the Virtual Tour Profit webinar. He was able to sell Google My Business 360° Virtual Tours as his lower-end product tier, and he upsold lead generation as a service. He recently closed a $10,000 contract combining his skills.

I taught him how to create lead generation campaigns, and I recorded the videos of those coaching calls and added it inside the program with VTPS. VTPS is designed to build a VR digital media agency, and if you join, you'll be able to see all the business models inside. Plus you get access to the community as we share cutting-edge selling frameworks and build out this business together.

I also want to note, I got a message from Ron that he was able to sell a $60,000 bulk package to a real estate office that included virtual tours, street view tours, and marketing services. Pretty cool deal to be able to go from $0 - $60,000 in revenue!

What's next?

THE VIRTUAL FOR PROFIT WEBINAR

www.virtualtourprofit.com

I highly recommend going to virtualtourprofit.com and watching the free webinar there. It's about an hour to 1.5 hours long, and it's extremely helpful to get you started from zero to become an expert and get your first sale. I will go through some examples of how to create virtual tours. I show you how to use our CloudPano virtual tour software to sell virtual tours as a service. Also, we detail in the webinar, VTPS - The Virtual Profit System.

What's inside VTPS? Why is it so important?

Why do members have so much success?

VTPS is a community and group environment where we build the business together through coaching, training, software, and technology. We join on weekly calls and we help each other grow our businesses.

The most value you can get from a program is congruency. Learn what is working now. Don't waste time on trying things out, building the website, or trying to figure out your pitch to each niche. Just ask the elite community, see what they're doing, and then iterate on what's **already working**. Get started today by watching the webinar at:

www.virtualtourprofit.com

Even if you don't join VTPS, you'll get a ton of value from the webinar. Also, if you want to read more details about our thesis and philosophy about this VR digital media agency, check out the specific website:

virtualtourprofit.com/apply

When you go there, you'll be able to look at VTPS and book a call with our team. Our mission is to help your business grow! The more money you make, the more success you have, the longer you will stay a member of CloudPano. YOUR success is OUR success!

YOUR CALL TO ACTION

I hope that this book has been helpful to you. I hope it's inspired you to get started and gives you more ideas to scale your existing business.

Come join our community. Check us out at virtualtourprofit.com. Let's get started together.

I'm excited for you and I'm excited to be involved in your entrepreneurial journey.

With love,

Zach Calhoon

Bonus

As a free bonus for purchasing this book, I made a 7 Day Quick Start Video Series. Inside this 7 day video series you will learn…

Day 1 – Pre-selling Your First Virtual Tour

Day 2 – How To Leverage The Power Of CloudPano

Day 3 – The 6 Figure Automation Funnel

Day 4 – Professional 360° Photography, Editing and Post Processing

Day 5 – Case Study: Making Your First $200,000 In 3

Months With Virtual Tours

Day 6 – The Subscription Selling Framework

Day 7 – How To Reverse Engineer Your Next $400,000 In Revenue

> To get instant access to this free bonus, visit here:
>
> blog.cloudpano.com/7-day-quick-start/

See you there!

www.ingramcontent.com/pod-product-compliance
Lightning Source LLC
Chambersburg PA
CBHW060838220526
45466CB00003B/1153